RUTGERS UNIVERSITY STUDIES IN PSYCHOLOGY

NUMBER ONE

AMERICAN PSYCHOLOGY
BEFORE WILLIAM JAMES

American Psychology Before William James

BY JAY WHARTON FAY

*I hold it a noble task to rescue from oblivion those
who deserve to be eternally remembered.*

PLINY THE YOUNGER

RUTGERS UNIVERSITY PRESS

NEW BRUNSWICK · NEW JERSEY · 1939

BF
108
.U5
F3
1939

150.973

Fay

PREFACE

THE history of psychology in America has never been
written. In an address delivered in 1898, J. M. Cattell
asserted that "the history of psychology here prior to
1880 could be set forth as briefly as the alleged chapter on
snakes in a certain natural history of Iceland—'There are
no snakes in Iceland.' " [1] The neatness of the witticism and
the authority of the speaker, combined with the general
reticence of the historians of psychology, [2] has contrived
to invest some two hundred and fifty years of American
thought with the obscurity of the dark ages. J. Mark
Baldwin, quoted literally by the German historian Klemm,
remarks that "early American psychology was written by
theologians or educators or both in the same person," [3]
and dismisses it with this laconic note. In a half dozen
pages of his valuable and scholarly three-volume work,
G. S. Brett manages to single out the least important
things in early American psychology for supercilious comment, pokes fun at authors whose works were never referred to by any of their compatriots, and misses all the
significant events of the rich and varied American past.
W. B. Pillsbury allows three pages to the period, while
E. G. Boring intentionally limits his profound study to
the history of experimental psychology, and J. C. Flugel
restricts his treatment to the last hundred years. In 1929,
Gardner Murphy re-echoes the general impression in his
statement that "prior to 1880, the only important Ameri-

can contributions were a few articles by James during the decade of the 'seventies.' " [4]

The neglect of the period by historians of psychology is further aggravated by the absorbing current interest in what is called "scientific psychology," and by a corresponding antipathy to anything that smacks of philosophy. This prejudice against speculative philosophy has not operated to prevent genuine historical scholarship in European psychology, and should not be allowed to stifle research into the development of psychology on American soil, where the early attempts at a science of the human mind were no more metaphysical than the contemporary essays in Great Britain and on the continent of Europe.

Interesting and significant studies have been made in early American philosophy, but such authorities as M. M. Curtis, A. L. Jones, L. van Becelaere, I. Woodbridge Riley, and H. S. Townsend have failed to lay any particular stress on the evolution of psychological ideas. [5]

Psychology in the strict etymological sense of the "science of the soul" is defunct. It was moribund in 1886, when John Dewey defined psychology as "the science of the facts or phenomena of self," [6] although in the same year James McCosh, and two years later, David Jayne Hill, made the last desperate effort to maintain the original definition. It was dead and buried in 1890, when William James consecrated a chapter in his epoch-making work to the passing of the soul. The "psyche" lingers on in a single anachronistic work, "Maher's Psychology," the standard text in the Catholic schools, in which Father Maher claims to represent a psychology "that has already survived four and twenty centuries, and has had more influence on human thought and human language than all

other psychologies together." [7] *The discipline which has
replaced the old psychology is still in its birth throes. It
is clearly a biological science with strong leanings towards
physiology and neurology. It repudiates its philosophical
antecedents, but, like metaphysics and unlike other sciences, it is marked by a division into warring sects. The
present situation is so chaotic that recent surveys of the
schools, such as those of R. S. Woodworth, C. E. Ragsdale
and Edna Heidbreder, attempt to untangle the maze with
obvious strain and with indifferent success.* [8]

*The new science is not coterminous with the old. It has
put objective and experimental methods to work in a limited portion of the field occupied by the obsolete philosophical psychology. For the rest, it has evaded problems
of vital importance that cannot be met by its technique,
or has frankly taken over terms, data, and conclusions
without realizing it, or at least without acknowledging its
obligations. This becomes increasingly clear as one studies
the contributions of the early American psychology.*

*The title of the present study indicates its limits. It
definitely terminates with the publication of James' "Principles of Psychology" in 1890. Up to this point the essential facts in the development of American psychology are
presented and evaluated in the light of contemporary
European psychology, and not according to criteria set up
by the science of today with essentially different aims,
techniques and objectives.*

*It should be noted that the term "American Psychol-
ogy" is chosen for its convenience to indicate psychology
in America, and especially psychology as developed by
American writers. It does not imply that psychology has
any national peculiarities. In the same way, "American"*

will be understood to refer to the British colonies in North America, and later to the United States.

Grateful acknowledgment is hereby made to the library staff at Rutgers University, and especially to Mr. G. A. Osborn, as well as to Dr. E. S. Worcester and the staff of the Sage Library, and to Dr. W. W. Rockwell of the Library of Union Seminary. Mr. Robert Bierstedt of Columbia University has read the entire text and made numerous and helpful criticisms.

Jay Wharton Fay

New Brunswick, New Jersey
April, 1939

TABLE OF CONTENTS

AMERICAN PSYCHOLOGY
BEFORE WILLIAM JAMES

THE PSYCHOLOGICAL HERITAGE OF THE PURITAN FATHERS

Limits of the Period Selected for Study

PSYCHOLOGY in America began in 1640 when Henry Dunster assumed the presidency of Harvard College. Psychology had not yet emerged from philosophy as a distinct discipline, and did not even have a name,[1] but its principles in so far as they were formulated or implied in the thought of the time may be recovered from the courses in Philosophy, Ethics and Divinity which Dunster set up in imitation of those with which he was familiar in the English Universities. Between this point and the publication of William James' "Principles of Psychology" in 1890 lies the neglected period of American psychology, the development and significance of which form the subject of this study.

From its inception in the curriculum offered to the first class at Harvard to the opening of the modern era, heralded by the appearance of James' "Principles," three periods may be distinguished, marked off by our two great armed conflicts, the Revolution and the Civil War. From the character of psychological thought in the first era, it may be designated the Period of Theology and Moral Philosophy, and the psychology taught under various rubrics may be characterized as traditional English scholasticism. It is dramatically interrupted by the arrival in 1714

3

of a copy of Locke's "Essay concerning Human Understanding," which with other contributing factors inaugurated an epoch corresponding closely to the British Enlightenment.

As soon as the country had recovered from the disorganization incident to the Revolution and the establishment of the Constitution, the Scottish philosophy of Thomas Reid and Dugald Stewart made its appearance in America, and dominated academic psychology until the time of Ladd, James and Baldwin. It was of the greatest importance to the end of the second period of American psychology, which falls between the Revolution and the Civil War, and which may be called the Period of Intellectual Philosophy. At first Reid and Stewart were studied in imported or reprinted texts, but in 1827, the publication of the first systematic text of psychology in the English language marks the beginning of an era of American textbooks, and divides the period into two parts, the first of which may appropriately bear the name of the parent philosophy, while the second indicates the rise of American scholarship.

The third period of some thirty years, extending from the Civil War to the publication of James' "Principles," may be designated the Period of British and German Influence. It is characterized by a growing dependence on British associationism, the gradual acceptance of the evolutionary theories of Darwin and Spencer, and the rapidly maturing interest in German psycho-physics and physiological psychology. Its close is marked by the work of Dewey, Ladd and Baldwin, who with James belong to the group which effected the transition to the spirit of the present.

The chronological outline of American psychology before 1890 is then as follows:

AMERICAN PSYCHOLOGY FROM 1640 TO 1890 (250 YEARS)

I. *Period of Theology and Moral Philosophy*, 1640-1776 (136 years)
   1. English Scholastic Education, 1640-1714
   2. The American Enlightenment, 1714-1776
II. *Period of Intellectual Philosophy*, 1776-1861 (85 years)
   1. The Scottish Philosophy, 1776-1827
   2. American Textbooks, 1827-1861
III. *Period of British and German Influence*, 1861-1890 (29 years)

It is obvious that these divisions are somewhat arbitrary, and that the overlapping familiar to students of human culture will be found here as in every phase of the history of thought. English scholastic education continued in some quarters for years after the arrival of Locke; Locke's "Essay" was a text in the colleges after the introduction of the Scottish philosophy; Reid, Stewart, Brown and Hamilton were a powerful influence in many academic circles during the whole of the third period; and British and German influences continued to be felt while American psychology was asserting a relative independence in the period beyond the close of this study. The two wars however do represent violent breaks in American culture, and the years chosen to subdivide the periods are marked by striking and significant events in the history of psychology in America.

The Mind of the Puritan Fathers

The first difficulty in the study of early American psychology is the reconstruction of the Puritan mind, a problem set up by Professor H. W. Schneider in a book of that name,[2] and characterized by him as impossible of solution by a twentieth-century scholar.

"His was a world into which we cannot enter, even in imagination. . . The materials with which men worked, the physical environment, the measure of knowledge of the world about them, were so totally different from those which we know that we must content ourselves with observing and recording the contrast." [3]

The difficulty is exaggerated in the case of psychology, because the science had not yet taken shape, and ideas which belong properly to that field are disguised and hidden beneath a theological terminology that is most misleading. Interminable discussions of "predestination" will be found to involve conceptions of the will, and the momentous question of "original sin" is weighted with considerations of heredity and the transmission of original and acquired characteristics. Admitting that one cannot feel himself or think himself into the Puritan mind with its peculiar interests and prepossessions, it is nevertheless necessary to ascertain just what it contained in the way of knowledge and belief in matters which we now term psychological.

The problem is localized in Puritan New England. The South did not have a college until the close of the seventeenth century, and may be disregarded for the purpose of this initial investigation. The same applies to the Middle Colonies. In the North, the Pilgrim Fathers were engaged in a life and death struggle for the first decade of their settlement, and it is not until the arrival of the Puritans to found the Massachusetts Bay Colony that we find a group sufficiently large and stable to make provision for higher education. Twenty thousand of these Puritans came to America in one decade, but then the stream of immigration fell off and the colony had no further supply of educated men from the mother country for many years. This meant an unfortunate cultural isolation.

"With the passing of the immigrant generation, a narrow provincialism settled down upon the commonwealth of Massachusetts Bay. Not a single notable book appeared; scarcely a generous figure emerged from the primitive background." [4]

"The freshening airs had ceased to blow, and there was none of that frequent contact with the culture of the Old World that there was in the South. . . The intellectual life that remained came to be pedantic and narrow rather than humane and broad, with both conscience and thrift operating against much that is valuable in social life and in the arts." [5]

The mind with which we are concerned is that of the university man of 1640, filled with the interests of his time and class, trained by the methods and limited within the intellectual horizons of Oxford and Cambridge, and relatively untouched by the rapid rise of the enlightenment in his native land. The English curriculum at the beginning of the seventeenth century was a direct evolution of that of the medieval universities. Aristotle practically dominated the course of study. The new learning and the beginnings of modern science had very little effect on the aims, curriculum and procedure of the universities, and still less on the colonists.

"The emigrants had no considerable part in the higher intellectual life of the age; the great artistic passions of Shakespeare and Milton touched them not at any point. Bacon's contribution to the art of finding truth did not belong to them. Men may live in the same time without being intellectual contemporaries." [6]

Copernican astronomy, Newtonian physics, the materialism of Hobbes, the invigorating thinking of Descartes and Locke, have no place on this horizon. These influences reached America in 1714, and belong to the later development of American thought.

Many of the Puritans belonged to an educated class. There was a higher percentage of university men in the Massachusetts Bay colony than in all England at the time.

"The proportion of learned men among them in those early days was extraordinary. It is probable that between the years 1630 and 1690 there were in New England as many graduates of Cambridge and Oxford as could be found in any population of similar size in the mother-country. At one time, during the first part of the period, there was in Massachusetts and Connecticut a Cambridge graduate for every 250 inhabitants, besides sons of Oxford not a few." [7]

They had been brought up on Ptolemaic astronomy, Aristotelian physics, Ciceronian philosophy and Biblical chronology. The world was created in 4004 B.C., on October 23, to be precise, and the universe was a "snug little place, and the earth occupied its center both in space and in importance." [8] The first man had been created perfect, but had fallen from grace and left to all his posterity the taint of his sin. The Biblical narrative was inspired, but many items not covered in its account of the world and man were treated with almost equal authority by Plato and Aristotle and admirably summarized by Cicero. The Greek and Latin classics were the last word in culture, and were intensively studied in the universities. Aristotle's contributions to science shaped the course of study.

"Our universities were founded when the Aristotelic philosophy was the dominant, or rather the exclusive, system, and the parts distributed to the different classes in the faculty of Arts or Philosophy, were regulated by the contents of certain of the Aristotelic books, and by the order in which they were studied. . . Aristotle's treatise On the Soul being (along with his lesser treatises on Memory and Reminiscence, on Sense and its Objects, etc.) included in the Parva Naturalia, and he, having declared that the consideration of the soul was part of the philosophy of nature, the science of Mind was always treated along with Physics. The professors of Natural Philosophy have, however, long abandoned the philosophy of mind, and this branch has been, as more appropriate to their departments, taught both by the Professors of Moral Philosophy and by the Professors of Logic and Metaphysics." [9]

In Aristotle's "De Anima" will be found much of the psychological thought of 1640. As Ebbinghaus says,

"In the fourth century before our era that giant thinker, Aristotle, built it [psychology] up into an edifice comparing very favorably with any other science of that time. But this edifice stood without undergoing any noteworthy change or extension, well into the eighteenth or even the nineteenth century." [10]

But Plato had also had a new lease of life, and Cambridge especially was saturated with Platonic philosophy, so-called. All this makes up "the garbled and antiquated mixture of scholastic Platonism and Calvinistic theology," [11] through which, as in a glass darkly, the Puritan looked at life and the human soul. The story of the rise, systematization, and transmission of the basic concepts of psychology is told in the standard histories. To summarize it briefly here, it is the science of a Platonic soul, endowed with Aristotelian faculties, Christianized by St. Paul and St. Augustine, systematized by Thomas Aquinas, divorced from the Catholic Church by Luther and Calvin, and transmitted, enmeshed in various philosophic disciplines, to our forefathers through the Protestant Colleges of Oxford and Cambridge.

At this point the history of psychology in America begins.

CHAPTER ONE

THE PERIOD OF THEOLOGY AND MORAL PHILOSOPHY

English Scholastic Education, 1640-1714

I. CONDITIONS IN THE COLONIES

A BRIEF survey of colonial conditions will account for the insignificance of higher education and consequently of psychology in the period. The population was small, scattered and almost exclusively rural. The settlers had to work hard,[1] and were harassed with frequent wars with the Indians and with almost constant participation in the American side of the armed conflicts of the mother country.

The religion of the colonists was mainly Protestant and Calvinistic, with a sprinkling of Catholics in the Middle Colonies, and a large Church of England group in the South. Theology was the dominant intellectual interest. From the establishment of the first printing press in 1639, a flood of sermons and religious tracts deluged the New World.[2] Communication however was difficult and travel between the colonies rare.

The Puritans made prompt preparations for elementary education, and the need for preparation of ministers of the Gospel led to the founding of the first college,[3] modeled after Magdalene College at Cambridge, a Puritan institution in which many of the New England colonists,

11

including John Harvard, had studied. For the first fifty years the President of Harvard College did all the teaching, and the student body rarely exceeded twenty.

In 1693, the Virginia Colony followed the example of Massachusetts with William and Mary College, a copy of Oxford, but not differing essentially from Harvard in its instruction. As Tyler says,

"We must not be misled by its imposing name. It was called a college; but during its earlier years it was only a boarding school for very young boys in very rudimental studies." [4]

Towards the end of the period Yale was founded,[5] receiving its traditions and practices together with its faculty from Harvard. It was an event in the history of Yale that marks the close of the period.

2. AMERICAN PSYCHOLOGY BETWEEN 1640 AND 1714

There is not a single product of American scholarship in any field whatever in the period between 1640 and 1714, as might be inferred from the analysis of conditions in the colonies.

"The condition of learning (as well as everything else) was very low in these times, indeed much lower than in the earlier time while those yet lived who had had their education in England and first settled the country. These were now gone off the stage, and their sons fell greatly short of their acquirements, as through the necessity of the times they could give but little attention to the business of education. . .

"There was nothing but the scholastic cobwebs of a few little English and Dutch systems. . . They heard indeed in 1714 . . . of a new philosophy that of late was all in vogue, and of such names as Descartes, Boyle, Locke and Newton, but they were cautioned against thinking anything of them, because the new philosophy, it was said, would soon bring in a new divinity and corrupt the pure religion of the country. . .

"Indeed there was no such thing as any books of learning to be had in these times under a 100 or 150 years old, such as the first settlers of the country brought with them 70 or 80 years before, and *some few used to make synopses or abridgments of these old scholastic systems.*" [6]

In 1714, *Samuel Johnson,*[7] later to become the first President of King's College, then eighteen years old and a tutor at Yale, made such an abridgment. His notebook contains these words: "November 11, 1714, Finitum Opus, Thanksgiving Day's Night," and below in parentheses was later added: "And by next Thanksgiving, November 16, 1715, I was wholly changed to the New Learning. See Tother Red Book." [8]

John Locke had arrived. "Tother Red Book" is the first fruits of the American Enlightenment. But before examining it, we may estimate the psychological thought of the first period by analyzing the content of Johnson's "abridgment of the old scholastic system."

Like Aristotle, Johnson makes psychology a part of Physics, which is defined as conversant with those things which arise and are produced not by art but by nature.[9] Universal rules are brought together by the light of the sacred Scriptures, human reason, sense-perception, induction and experience. These rules must be disposed according to a method consistent with reason and the order of creation. The Peripatetics do not follow such a method, because they follow not Moses but Aristotle, and learn their philosophy from the heathen master rather than from the sacred pages.

Adam,[10] our first parent, was endowed with illustrious

wisdom before the fall, but after this unfortunate event, such sparks of it as survived were kept alive in the philosophical schools of the Hebrews. Later, the Greeks, notably Pythagoras, Socrates, Plato, and Aristotle, cultivated philosophy, and from Greece it spread into Italy and the countries of northern Europe, where not a few of the greatest men were found, "for their teaching was Christian." The principal philosophical schools were the Platonic, the Peripatetic, and the Eclectic. The leader of the Eclectics was Ramus, at whose feet, as it were, followed Richardson and Ames, "the greatest of them all," and "we follow Ames."

Among the phenomena of natural physics are *spirits*, defined as unchanging, living, and intelligent natures, and divided into two classes, angels and rational souls.[11] On account of the union of the body and the rational soul, the author proposes to treat of the soul later in connection with man, but his manuscript breaks off, and the subject is resumed in the Encyclopaedia, after 806 propositions devoted to technology, generation, types, logic, grammar, rhetoric, arithmetic, geometry, and physics.

The spirit has three *faculties*, life, intellect, and will.[12] *Life* is defined as the act of the vivifier in the vivified by the union of both; the *intellect* is the faculty of the spirit by which it knows and judges objects, its acts being apprehension, thought, memory, and recollection; *will* is the faculty by which objects perceived and judged by the intellect are pursued and avoided. Its acts are volition and the opposite.

After inanimate bodies are disposed of, *animate mixtures* are taken up, and defined as possessing a soul, their members being soul and body. The *body* is the member so organized as to be suited to the operations and functions of the soul; the *soul*, on the other hand, being the member which is the principle of those operations. Animated beings may have one or more souls. Plants have a *vegetative soul*, whose operations are appetite, attraction, retention, digestion, nutrition, growth, excretion, and procreation. Each of these faculties is defined, and we come next to animals, animate beings furnished with several souls, vegetative, motive and sensitive. The animal has members and species, its members also being body and soul. The parts of the body are named and briefly described, and we come at last by this process of inexorable logic to the discussion of the soul.

The *sensitive soul* is the elemental spirit which is the principle of sensation, appetite, and motion, these being its three faculties. The *external senses* are sight, hearing, smell, taste, and touch. Their modes are being awake and being asleep, the former being the excitation of the external senses, the latter their bondage. Each sense requires an organ, an object, and a congruous medium. The *internal senses* are those by which the animal perceives internally the objects perceived externally and judges them, their acts being imagination, thought, and memory.

The *appetite* is the faculty by which the animal spirits are excited, and is either an emotion, a movement, respiration, or beating of the pulse. *Emotions* are animal movements arising out of the pursuit of good and the avoidance of evil. They are classified into two main groups: emotions of approval (pleasurable, the animal spirits coming *from* the heart), or of disapproval (painful, the animal spirits in this case going *to* the heart). Pleasure arises from the perception of an agreeable object, and its emo-

tions are joy, hope, and love. Pain is derived from the perception of a disagreeable object, and its emotions are
either simple, as madness, pity, and fear, or mixed, as
anger and jealousy.

As to species, animals are either brutes or men, the
former being only sentient and irrational, the latter having a *rational soul*. Man's properties are speech (his system of mental symbols by articulate sounds), his ability
to laugh (his sign of joy), and weeping (his sign of
grief).

"All animals both man and beast are male and female, by
nature stronger or weaker. All these natural beings are orderly
assembled in a round whole which is the world." [13]

This was the corpus of psychological doctrine in America in 1714. Sad as it is, it probably represents pretty well
the state of knowledge and belief in Europe also, at the
time when Hobbes, Descartes, and Locke began to apply
Baconian methods to the investigation of the human soul.
It was Plato shorn of his poetry, Aristotle without his
breadth and acuteness of observation and his carefully
qualified conclusions, Thomas Aquinas without his logical
subtlety. From these rude beginnings American psychology traveled the long road to William James in less than
two centuries. One turns with relief to the contributions
of the Enlightenment.

The American Enlightenment, 1714-1776

I. PROGRESS OF EUROPEAN THOUGHT

The cultural isolation of New England from 1640 to
1714 kept the colonists in ignorance of the development

of European thought during the sixteenth century. The new scientific attitude announced by Bacon led almost immediately to the work of Hobbes and Locke in England, of Descartes and Malebranche in France, of Spinoza in Holland, and of Leibniz in Germany.

When cultural relations were resumed with the mother country through a fresh wave of immigration in the eighteenth century, the progress of European thought was promptly reflected on this side of the Atlantic. The conclusions drawn by Berkeley and Hume from the premises of Locke, the materialistic psychology of Hartley, the evolution of the Cartesian philosophy into the sensationalism of Condillac and Bonnet and the materialism of d'Holbach and la Mettrie, and the work of Christian Wolff in Germany, all had a repercussion, favorable or unfavorable in the writings and thought of American philosophers. The revolt of Thomas Reid from the idealism of Berkeley and the skepticism of Hume reached this country at the end of the period, and proved to be of immense importance in shaping future developments on American soil.

2. CONDITIONS IN THE COLONIES

While the population grew rapidly during the period, it was still largely rural, and the cities were mere villages. The colonists were continually engaged in a series of wars with the French and the Indians. Communication was still difficult, the mails slow, and the postage rates exorbitantly high.

With the influx of new ideas came the invasion of Deism.

"Rationalism was in the air, and although it might be excluded from the minister's study, it spread its subtle infection through the mass of the people. . . The word Arminian sprinkles more liberally the pages of controversial literature, indicating the nature of the attack against Calvinism." [14]

Private and public libraries increased in size and numbers, and the growing population and a rising intellectual interest demanded an expansion of the educational program. Three colleges were not enough.

"About the middle of the 18th century and apparently in response to a single and common interest, the Colonies of Pennsylvania, of New Jersey, and of New York set themselves to the establishment of colleges for the better education of the young men in their various communities." [15]

A little later the list of the colonial colleges was completed with Brown (1754), Rutgers (1766) and Dartmouth (1769). In spite of the expansion the program was totally inadequate for a population of nearly four million.

3. AMERICAN PSYCHOLOGY FROM 1714-1776

Between 1714 and the Revolution four American scholars made indirect contributions to psychology, *William Brattle* at Harvard, *Samuel Johnson* at King's College, *Thomas Clap* at Yale, and *Jonathan Edwards*. Brattle wrote the first textbook on Logic, Johnson published the first American work in Philosophy, Clap fathered a text in Ethics, and Edwards made a notable contribution to Theology. Towards the end of the period John Witherspoon was lecturing on Moral Philosophy at Princeton, introducing the point of view of the Scottish philosophy. But his lectures were interrupted by the war, and when they were resumed, Reid and Stewart had arrived. "Witherspoon's Works" were published in 1800, and his ideas are best taken up in the next period together with the philosophy which they most resembled.

a. *William Brattle* [16]

"Logic was the main study in all the higher institutions, and the logic bequeathed by the schoolmen meant merely incessant practice in the art of dialectical disputation as a means of acquiring universal truth. . . This highly regarded 'Aristotelian method' had for ages retarded the advance toward larger learning and broader views." [17]

The first texts in Logic in the Colonial Colleges were those of Ramus and Burgersdicius.[18] Then came a manuscript text by Charles Morton, brought with him to America from his private school in England.[19] This was followed by Brattle's book, which, after forty-five years of use in manuscript form, was finally printed and became the first work of any kind by an American emphasizing psychological ideas.

The full title of the work is

Compendium/ Logicae/ Secundum Principia/ D. Renati Cartesii/
Plerumque Efformatum/ et/ Catechistice Propositum [20]

It is a formal little work of sixty octavo pages, written in Latin in question and answer form.

"Aside from the fact that it shows the influence of Cartesianism in America, there is nothing memorable about the book. It is an elementary text, rather formal in character, including large portions given to what we now consider subject matter of psychology—perception, memory, imagination, etc." [21]

Jones paraphases part of the Prolegomena and indicates the contents of Part I:

"The use of Logic is like that of a medicine to the body; it aids in freeing the mind from the defects of ignorance and forgetfulness, doubt and error, obscurity and the like. The rules of certainty given are first, nothing is to be admitted as true so long as it includes anything of doubt; second, we should beware of trusting too much to the senses; third, what we perceive we perceive by the mind alone; and fourth, that is true which we perceive clearly and distinctly. Part I deals with ideas and the simple contemplation of things which are considered under the heads of perception, objects of perception, primary and secondary, and relations." [22]

The author follows the fourfold classification (De Perceptione, De Iudicio, De Discursu, De Methodo) invented by Ramus, continued by Gassendi, and adopted by the Port Royal Logic (1662), with which he was probably familiar. Like the Port-Royalists he tends to expand Logic beyond the Aristotelian limits and to make it include a good deal of Cartesian psychology. This tendency was further developed by Isaac Watts, whose Logic (1725), already in use at Harvard by 1746, superseded Brattle's, and itself gave way to a text written by Levi Hedge in 1816, also containing liberal portions of psychology.

b. *Early Echoes of John Locke*

Between Johnson's Old Encyclopaedia of 1714 and the Elementa Philosophica we have a revised Encyclopaedia, dated 1715, and a Logic (1720), which together with some correspondence with his colleague, Daniel Brown, show the influence of Bacon and Locke, but do not yet give a hint of the idealism which was soon to come into Johnson's philosophy through the writings of and personal contact with Bishop George Berkeley.[23]

As these Lockian ideas remained quite permanently in Johnson's system they may be summarized here.

EXTRACTS FROM SAMUEL JOHNSON'S REVISED ENCYCLOPAEDIA AND LOGIC

"*Physic* [24] is in general the science or art of searching after and discovering the nature of things, scil. of all created substances, and to this mathematics is greatly subservient and useful, for the phenomena of nature are many of them best solved by mathematics. Now as this science comprehends the natures of the university of all created substances, *spirits as well as bodies, and the qualities, powers, and affections of them both,* there are therefore many particular sciences comprehended under it, namely, in particular

"1. The heavens, angels and human souls being above the sphere of matter and motion present themselves to be the subject of the science *metaphysics* or *pneumatics,* etc.[25]

"My *method* [26] shall consist in giving a plain and historical account of our several intellectual powers and prescribing rules for their direction. . .

"All our *intellectual powers* may be referred to these three, scil. *apprehension, judgment* and *reason.* For the general act of intellection may be termed *perception.* . . Sometimes we perceive and take notice only of one object at once being singly represented to our understanding. This is called *simple apprehension.* Sometimes we perceive the relation between two objects laid together; this is called *judgment.* And lastly sometimes we perceive the relation between three objects or between two by the modification of a third, and this we call *reason.* Thus I make the three general distinctions of our *faculties.* . . The form of this simple apprehension is *idea,* that image of thought of any thing immediately set before the mind. . .

"*All ideas come into the mind either by sensation or reflec-*

tion. By *sensation,* I understand that notice the mind takes of the objects without it by the intervention of the five senses, those inlets of ideas, the eyes, ears, nose, palate and indeed all parts of the body. . . And it may be here observed that it is by these sensible qualities variously affecting the senses, and through them variously insinuating themselves into the mind, that our minds are first put into action, for though they act freely enough when once they have these materials to work upon, yet till they are some measure stored and furnished with the characters of these sensible qualities, with these first materials of thinking about which they are employed, we cannot conceive of any action of them at all. By *reflection* I understand the notice which the mind takes of its operations. . . Hereby we have the ideas of thinking, perceiving, apprehending, knowing, reasoning, loving, hating, hoping, fearing, willing, and willing choosing and refusing, etc. And these two, sensation and reflection, are the origin of all our ideas, and there are no ideas how remote soever from them but what may be by them easily accounted for and referred to them.

"All the *ideas* that our minds are by these two sources possessed with are either *simple* or *complex.* . . These simple ideas with which our minds are stored . . . come into them by one sense . . . or by more senses than one . . . or by reflection only . . . or, lastly, by all ways of sensation and reflection. Complex ideas are such as consist of a combination of various simple ideas in the mind. . .

"The soul has a power to continue the idea for a while under its view and this may be called *retention.* Again it has a power whereby after the disappearing of an idea it can recollect and call it to mind again. Now the capacity of the mind to do this is its *memory,* and the actual doing it is its *remembrance,* which differs from the first apprehension of the idea only in this, that the mind now perceives it with a consciousness of having perceived it before. . .

"And in contemplating its ideas sometimes the mind only just attends to its ideas without any very strong application, and this is called its *attention*, again at other times it applies itself with very great strength and vigor to the consideration of them even so as to be deaf to all the solicitations of sense, and this is called *intention* or *study*. And when the mind is thus intent upon its ideas, it has a power whereby it can add many simple or complex ideas together, or having any complex idea, it can subtract from it what part or parts it pleases and so increase or diminish it and make it greater or less. Again it can alter the situation of its parts by transposing them and modify them according to its pleasure. In short, the power of the mind upon its simple ideas is much the same as a man's power is upon matter, for though we can't create the least particular or atom, yet we can modify it how we please in many cases.

"Moreover the mind . . . can consider various numbers of individuals, what they have that is proper and peculiar to themselves . . . and what simple ideas there are in common among them, and separate them by *abstraction* and combine them under some general name. . .

"And then finally sometimes we may observe that remissness in our minds that they will suffer a long train of ideas pass through them without taking any great matter of notice of any connection between them, and this the French call *reverie*, and that we can form to ourselves what exotic notions we please that have nothing in nature that answers them . . . and this is the mere work of the *imagination*. And in *dreaming*, ideas seem to jostle together many times without any design of the mind at all or very little, by which odd fancies arise in it which had no resemblance to anything that ever was or ever will be. . .

"But however various these and the like *powers and operations of the mind* are, yet they *are* still *confined within the compass of those simple ideas of sensation and reflection.*"

A comparison of these statements with those of the previous formulations will reveal the intimate, even verbal, influence of John Locke, and lead us to wonder at the astonishing advance that the youthful philosopher had made in a single year. At about the same time Jonathan Edwards too had come upon Locke, whose writings are reflected in his Notes on Mind.[27] Edwards leaped almost immediately from Locke's propositions to the idealistic conclusions which Berkeley was to draw from them in his Theory of Vision and Principles of Human Knowledge.[28] A few quotations will confirm the prompt and vigorous influence of Locke on the American philosophical mind.

EXTRACTS FROM JONATHAN EDWARDS' NOTES ON MIND

"TITLE. The Natural History of the Mental World, or of the Internal World: being a Particular Enquiry into the Nature of the Human Mind, with respect to both its Faculties—the Understanding and the Will—and its various Instincts, and Active and Passive Powers.

"*Introduction.* Concerning the two worlds—the External and the Internal: the External, the subject of Natural Philosophy; the Internal, our own Minds. How the knowledge of the latter is, in many respects, the most important. Of what great use, the true knowledge of this is; and of what dangerous consequences errors, here, are more than in the other.

Subjects to be handled in the Treatise on the Mind
[Here follow 56 numbered paragraphs, of which the following are selected to show the influence of Locke]

29. "*Sensation.* How far all the acts of the mind are from Sensation. All ideas begin from thence; and there can never be any idea, thought, or act of the mind, unless the mind first re-

ceived some ideas from Sensation, or some other way equivalent, wherein the mind is wholly passive in receiving them.

31. "Sensation. Whether all ideas, wherein the mind is merely passive, and which are received immediately without any dependence on Reflexion, are not ideas of Sensation, or External ideas. Whether there be any difference between them? Whether it be possible for the Soul of man, in like manner, to be originally, and without dependence on Reflexion, capable of receiving any other ideas than those of sensation, or something equivalent, and so some external idea?

43. *"Connection of Ideas.* Concerning the Laws by which Ideas follow each other, or call up one another, in which one thing comes into the mind after another, in the course of our thinking. How far this is owing to the Association of Ideas; and how far, to any Relations of Cause and Effect, or any other Relation, and whether the whole may not be reduced to these following: *Association of Ideas; Resemblance of some kind;* and that *Natural Disposition* in us, when we see any thing begin to be, to suppose it owing to a Cause.—Observe how these laws, by which one idea suggests and brings in another, are a kind of mutual attraction of ideas.—Concerning the importance, and necessity, of this mutual attraction and adhesion of ideas—how rarely our minds would serve us, if it were not for this. How the mind would be without ideas, except as suggested by the Senses. How far Reasoning, Contemplation, etc., depend on this.

51. "Whether all the Immediate Objects of the mind, are properly called *Ideas;* and what inconvenience and confusion arises from giving every Subjective thought that name. What prejudices and mistakes it leads to.

52. "In what respects *Ideas* or thoughts, and judgments, may be said to be *Innate,* and in what respect not.

53. "Whether there could have ever been any such thing as Thought, without External Ideas, immediately impressed by

God, either according to some law, or otherwise. Whether any Spirit or Angel, could have any thought, if it had not been for this. Here particularly explain what I mean by *External Ideas*.

54. "How *words* came to have such a mighty influence on thought, and judgment, by virtue of the Association of Ideas, or from Ideas being habitually tied to words."

Then come random thoughts, developing more elaborately the articles proposed for investigation. The following have again been chosen to show the influence of Locke. Edwards' psychology will be discussed in a later section.

11. "Well might Mr. Locke say, that identity of *person* consisted in identity of consciousness; for he might have said that identity of *spirit*, too, consisted in the same consciousness; for a mind or spirit is nothing else but consciousness, and what is included in it. The same consciousness is, to all intents and purposes, individually, the very same spirit, or substance; as much as the same particle of matter can be the same with itself, at different times. [Edwards changes his point of view in a subsequent note—72.]

41. "As there is a great foundation in Nature for those abstract ideas, which we call Universals; so there is great foundation in the common circumstances and necessities of mankind, and the constant method of things proceeding, for such a tying of simple modes together to the constituting of *mixed modes*.

42. "The agreement or similitude of *Complex ideas*, mostly consists in their precise identity, with respect to some third idea of some of the simples, they are compounded of . . .

43. "Many of our Universal ideas are not Arbitrary. The tying of them together, in Genera and Species, is not merely the calling of them by the same name, but such a union of them, that the consideration of one shall naturally excite the idea of others. . .

70. "That it is not Uneasiness, in our present circumstances,

that always determines the Will, as Mr. Locke supposes, is evident by this, that there may be an Act of the Will, in choosing and determining to forbear to act, or move, when some action is proposed to a man; as well as in choosing to act."

"The preceding articles were written as comments on the various subjects treated of, while the author was studying the Essay on the Human Understanding. It is not improbable that some of the later numbers were written while the author was a tutor in College." [29]

It is obvious that Edwards does not always agree with Locke even when he is getting ideas from him. Other thoughts, not quoted here, show how interested Edwards already was in the Will, and how he had already arrived at an astonishing position with respect to Idealism.

"No one, probably, will rise from a perusal of this early effort, without feeling a deep regret that the author did not devote an adequate portion of time to the completion of a plan, so well conceived, of what must have proved an able and profound Treatise on Mental Philosophy. In his Treatise on the Will, we have indeed one great division of this very work. From the unrivalled success of his researches in the investigation of that faculty, it appears deeply to be lamented, that he should not have found leisure, for a similar Essay on the Human Understanding." [30]

c. *Samuel Johnson, 1696-1772*

From his crude youthful summaries of scholastic philosophy, from his literal borrowings from Bacon and Locke, Samuel Johnson advanced through wide reading,[31] personal contact with George Berkeley,[32] and the exercise of a superior intelligence to the mature expression of the Elementa Philosophica, the "first textbook of Philosophy published in America." [33] His psychology will be given a full analysis here, as representing the high point of the eighteenth century in America. The order of topics adopted in Baldwin's Dictionary of Philosophy and Psychology [34] will be followed, as representing valid categories for the psychology that was just becoming obsolete at the close of the nineteenth century.

I. *General*

"Intelligent and active beings are called spirits, and that part of natural philosophy which treats of the nature of spirits is called metaphysics, or *pneumatology*, which

1. Treats of the nature and powers of our own souls, and then
2. Inquiries concerning other tribes of intelligences, and
3. Of the nature, attributes and operations of God . . . the father and original of all created spirits. (This is called Theology.) [35]

"PNEUMATOLOGY is the doctrine of spirits or created intelligences; and here we begin with our own souls, their powers and operations, both perceptive and active: and thence proceed to other intelligences whether good or bad: and by analogy we gradually rise to the best conceptions we are capable of, of the Deity, the Father, Creator and Lord of all. [36]

"The word *mind* or *spirit*, in general, signifies any intelligent active being; which notion we take from what we are conscious of in ourselves, who know that we have within us a principle of conscious perception, intelligence, activity and self-exertion; or rather, that each of us is a conscious, perceptive, intelligent, active and self-exerting being: and by reasoning and analogy from ourselves we apply it to other minds or intelligences besides or superior to us; and (removing all limitations and imperfections) we apply it even to that Great Supreme Intelligence. . . By the *human mind,* we mean that principle of sense, intelligence and free activity, which we feel within ourselves, or rather feel ourselves to be, furnished with those objects and powers, and under those confinements and limitations, under which it has pleased our great Creator to place us in this present state.[37]

"It is my *design* in the following essay, to trace out, in as short a compass as I can, the several steps of the mind of man, from the first impressions of sense, through the several improvements it gradually makes, till it arrives to that perfection and enjoyment of itself, which is the great end of our being. In order to which, it will first be expedient to define what we mean by the human mind, and to give some account of its various objects, powers, and operations, and the principles and rules by which they are to be conducted in attaining to the knowledge of truth. . .

"Making due reflections on the operations of our own minds, and the large extent of our intellectual faculties and their objects; their several distinct exertions, and their subserviency to each other; the free activity of our souls, and the various passions that put them on action for attaining our several ends; and the various ways wherein they exert themselves, and exercise their dominion over our bodies.[38]

"As I cannot conceive how the *true end of* my *being,* especially of that superior nature, which is the peculiar character of our species, can be answered merely by living this wretched, short and uncertain life, that is allotted to me here; so I am persuaded, that I am designed for some other and nobler condition of being hereafter, and cannot avoid having hopes full of immortality. . . Thus it appears, that the true and ultimate end of my being, can be nothing short of this; that I may be as happy as my condition will admit of here, and eternally and completely happy in the future state of my existence, in the enjoyment of God, and all that is good, and in the perfection of knowledge and virtue, which alone can render me capable thereof." [39]

In the Introduction to Philosophy, Johnson gives a "Catalogue of some of the most valuable Authors on each Part of Philosophy, proper to be read by the Students," [40] e.g.:

I. IN RATIONAL PHILOSOPHY.
   1. "On *Logic* and *Metaphysics,* read Ars Cogitandi, Le Clerc, Watts, Locke, Crousaz, Medicina Mentis by Welstead, Lord Bacon, Locke's Conduct of the Understanding." (Six other sections of bibliography.)
II. IN NATURAL PHILOSOPHY. (Six sections.)
III. IN MORAL PHILOSOPHY.
   1. "On *Pneumatology,* read Le Clerc's Pneumatologia, Locke's Human Understanding passim, Wollaston's Religion of Nature, Clarke's Letters to Dodwell and Leibniz, Malebranche, Descartes Metaphysics, Norris's Ideal World, Bp. Berkeley's New Theory of Vision, Principles of Human Knowledge, Dialogues et Tract. de Motu; Bp. Browne's Procedure and Extent of Human Understanding and divine Analogy; Shaftsbury's Philosophical Rhapsody; Watts's Philosophical Essays. (Fourteen other sections.)

II. *Anatomy and Physiology of the Nervous System*

The only advances made in this field since Aristotle, Hippocrates and Galen were negligible,[41] and had not reached Johnson, so that matter under this heading treats (as with Aristotle) of the connections of mind and body.

"We are, at present, spirits or minds connected with gross, tangible bodies, in such a manner, that as our bodies can perceive and act nothing but by our minds, so, on the other hand, our minds perceive and act by means of our bodily organs—which I conceive to be no other than a mere arbitrary constitution or establishment of Him that hath made us to be what we are . . . viz. that our bodies should be thus acted on by our minds, and that our minds should thus perceive and act by the organs of our bodies, and under such limitations as in fact we find ourselves to be attended with." [42]

III. *Sensation*

"Our minds may be said to be created mere tabulae rasae . . . they are no more authors to themselves of the objects of their perceptions, or the light by which they perceive them, than of the power of perceiving itself. . . All the notices we have in our minds derive to them originally from (or rather by means of) these two fountains, sense and consciousness. (p. 374.)

"By *sense*, we mean, those perceptions we have of objects ab extra, or by means of the several organs of our bodies. Thus . . . touch . . . sight . . . hearing . . . tasting . . . smelling. (p. 374.)

"In the perception of these ideas of objects of sense, we find our minds are merely passive, it not being in our power (supposing our organs rightly disposed and situated) whether we will see light and colors, hear sounds, etc. (p. 375).

"The immediate object of these our perceptions and actions we call ideas . . . any immediate object of the mind in thinking. . . Plato, indeed, by the word idea, understood the original exemplar of things, whether sensible or intellectual, in the eternal mind, conformable to which all things exist. . . But perhaps, for the more distinct understanding ourselves upon this subject, it may be best to confine the word idea to the immediate objects of sense and imagination, which was the original meaning of it, and to use the word notion or conception, to signify the objects or consciousness and pure intellect." (pp. 373-4.)

IV. *Characters of Consciousness*

"By consciousness is meant, our perception of objects ab extra, or from reflecting or turning the eye of our mind inward, and observing what passeth within itself; whereby we know that we perceive all those sensible objects and their connections, and all the pleasures and pains attending them, and all the powers and faculties of our minds employed about them. Thus I am conscious that I perceive light and colors, sounds, odors, sapors, and tangible qualities, with all the various combinations of them; and that of these, some give me, or rather are attended with pain or uneasiness, others with pleasure or ease, and the comfortable enjoyment of myself. (p. 377.)

"No sooner does any object strike the senses, or is received in our imagination, or apprehended by our understanding, but we are immediately conscious of a kind of intellectual light within us (if I may call it so) whereby we not only know that we perceive the object, but directly apply ourselves to the consideration of it, both in itself, its properties and powers, and as it stands related to all other things. . . This intellectual light I conceive of as it were a medium of knowledge, as sensible light is of sight; in both there is the power of perceiving, and the object perceived; and this is the medium by which I am enabled to know it. And this light is one, and common to all intelligent beings, and enlighteneth alike every man that cometh into the world, a Chinese or Japanese, as well as an European or American, and an angel as well as a man: by which they all at once see the same thing to be true or right in all places at the same time, and alike invariably in all times, past, present, and to come. (p. 379.)

"Now if it be asked, whence does this light derive . . . I answer . . . from the universal presence and action of the Deity, or a perpetual communication with the great father of lights. [Footnote references to Clarke, Norris, Malebranche and Cudworth.] . . . And from this intuitive intellectual light it is (as I conceive) that we derive what we call taste and judgment, and, with respect to morals, what we call the moral sense or the conscience, which are only a sort of quick intuitive sense or apprehension of the decent and amiable, of beauty and deformity, of true and false, and of right and wrong, or duty and sin: and it is the chief business of culture, art and instruction, to awaken it, and turn our attention to it, and assist us in making deductions from it. (pp. 379-80.)

"As by a spirit, which is also called a person, we mean a distinct, conscious, intelligent agent, so his identity consists in being conscious of a series of perceptions and actions that he knows to be his own and not another's, by which therefore he knows that he is the same person now with himself twenty or fifty years ago, which continued consciousness is his distinct individuating property. (pp. 397-8.)

"As I am certain from the perceptions and operations of my own mind that I am, or have a being; so I know that I am not a stock, a stone, or a tree. . . Nor yet am I a beast, a horse, a dog, or an ox, etc., for . . . they appear to have no notion of any thing but the objects of sense. . . These sensations, appetites and exertions, indeed, I find I have in common with them, but then I am conscious of vastly nobler powers and faculties than these. For I find I can reflect and look into my own mind. . . I can attend to the light of pure intellect. . . I can judge of true and false. . . I can excite imaginations and conceptions of things past or absent, and recollect them in my mind at pleasure . . . and am at liberty to suspend judging till I have carefully examined them, and to act, or not to act, in consequence of my deliberations, as I think fit. . . I can, moreover, in consequence of these abilities, contrive and project ends and means, and reasons of acting, and rules to act by, and foresee much of the events of my conduct. . . (p. 455.)

"And as I can look back and remember what I have been knowing to in my time; so I can imagine a time when I was not, and conceive a notion of a great number of ages and transactions before me, and of an endless succession of ages and transactions to come. . . All these are so many facts, and I am conscious and intuitively certain of them, if I look carefully within myself. And such are the properties of my soul or spirit, which is properly myself, my reasonable and active nature." (p. 456.)

V. *Cognition*

"I find moreover, that when I have had any perception or impression of sense, I retain a faint image of it in my mind afterwards, or have a kind internal sense or remembrance of it. . . This power of the mind is called *imagination* and *memory*, which implies a consciousness of the original impression. . . We are moreover conscious of a power whereby we can not only imagine things as being what they really are in nature, but can also join such parts and properties of things together, as never co-existed in nature . . . which must be referred to the imagination, but as influenced by the will.

"But besides these powers of sense and imagination, we are conscious of what is called the *pure intellect*, or the power of conceiving of abstracted or spiritual objects, and the relations between our several ideas and conceptions, and the various dispositions, exertions and actions of our minds, and the complex notions resulting from all these; of all which we cannot be properly said to have ideas, they being entirely of a different kind from the objects of sense and imagination, on which account I would rather call them notions or conceptions. . .

And of all these, and what relates to them, consists the entire spiritual or moral world. . .

"But in order the better to understand or conceive of these, it is necessary more particularly to pursue and explain these intellectual and active powers, whereof we are conscious within ourselves; such as 1. The *simple apprehension* of objects and their relations . . . 2. *Judging* of true or false . . . and 3. *Reasoning* or inferring one thing from another, and methodizing them according to their connections and order. (pp. 377-8.)

"Let us therefore proceed to define the several acts and objects of the pure intellect thus enlightened. And first, of the *simple apprehension* of objects or beings, and the various conceptions arising to our view from the consideration of their natures and affections, and their several relations, connections and dependencies, such as cause and effect, essence and existence, things possible and impossible, necessary and contingent, finite and infinite, perfect and imperfect, truth and good, beauty and harmony, substances and accidents, subjects and adjuncts, time and place, whole and parts, unity and multiplicity, number and order, identity and diversity, things agreeing and opposite, equal and unequal, like and unlike, denomination and definition, individuals and abstraction, kinds and sorts, bodies and spirits; and lastly, of metaphor and analogy from things sensible to things spiritual, and from things human to things divine. Of all which I shall treat in the order as they are here enumerated. . ." (Simple apprehension is treated at length in Ch. II, Schneider, II, pp. 381-404.)

Judgment, defined as that act of the mind "which affirms or denies one thing of another, and judges of true and false," and *Reasoning,* "that act of the mind which seeks reasons or arguments to prove the truth or falsehood of any proposition, and makes use of them to that purpose" are treated in Chapters III and IV (Logic). (Schneider, II, pp. 404-417.)

VI. *Affection*

In the preliminary discussion of the pure intellect, the affections are placed after Reasoning, in these words:

"To which succeed, Affecting or disaffecting them according as they appear good or bad, agreeable or disagreeable to us, i.e., attended with pleasure or uneasiness." (p. 378.)

"[The passions are defined as] such affections or disaffections, inclinations or aversions, as we experience in ourselves, upon feeling or expecting that pleasure or uneasiness with which any object is attended. And such is the law of union between our souls and bodies, that upon our being affected or disaffected towards any object, we are sensible of certain commotions and perturbations in our blood and spirits, corresponding and in proportion to those pleasing or displeasing apprehensions."

"The leading passion, and which seems in some degree to be at the bottom in all our passions, is what we call *admiration* or *wonder*, which in a high degree is called *astonishment*." (p. 418.)

A brief but clear account follows of love, joy, esteem, pity, compassion, desire and hope; of hate, grief, shame, contempt, terror and fear; of benevolence, complacence, gratitude, friendship, and malevolence, anger, resentment, envy and malice. (pp. 418-9.)

"These passions are natural to us, and, as such, must be considered as part of the frame of our natures . . . and therefore are so far from being evil in themselves, that they have the nature of good, as well as all our other faculties, and so, like the rest, become morally good or evil, according to the good or ill use we make of them. . . For the passions are, as it were, the wings of the soul, by which it is carried on with vehemence and impetuosity in its several pursuits; and, as it were, its springs, by which it is animated and invigorated in all its exertions." (p. 419.)

They must "be duly balanced one with another, and rightly governed and moderated in proportion to the real value and importance of their respective objects. . . One of the chief concerns in culture and education is, to discipline and moderate the passions, and to inure them to a ready submission to the dictates of reason and conscience." (p. 420. *See also* pp. 491-2.)

VII. *Conation and Movement*

In the general outline, conation is described as "Willing or nilling, choosing or refusing according as we affect or disaffect [objects of perception]," and a definite stand is taken on the moot question of the freedom of the will; which is defined as

"Liberty of acting, or forbearing to act in consequence of the judgment and choice we have made of them. . . Our will consists in freely resolving and determining ourselves to the one or the other, as they shall appear to our judgment; so our highest moral perfection consists in actually making a right judgment, what we ought to affect or disaffect, and to do and forbear; and in freely and habitually exerting ourselves in choosing and doing the one, and rejecting and forbearing the other, conformable thereunto. I say, freely; for freedom or liberty consisteth in having a power to act, or not to act, as we please, and consequently to suspend judgment or acting, till we have taken opportunity to make as deliberate and exact a judgment as ever we can; what is best for us in the whole, to do or forbear; as necessity, on the other hand, considered as opposed to liberty, implieth, that it is out of our power to suspend acting, or to do otherwise than we do, in which case there can be neither praise nor blame." (pp. 378, 421.)

Obligations are referred to the laws of self-love, self-preservation, and benevolence, and the law of reason and conscience is identified with the moral sense, as held by Shaftesbury, Hutcheson and Turnball. The springs of action are found in the passions.

VIII. *Higher Manifestations of Mind*

This section includes Logic, Science, Epistemology, Aesthetics, Ethics, and Religion, to each of which Johnson made contributions. His Logic is derived from Crousaz, the Port Royalists, and Isaac Watts. His Science is illustrated in a table inserted between the two parts of the Elementa Philosophica. (p. 449.) His Epistemology is based on Berkeley, Malebranche, and Norris, and is evolved out of pure Idealism.

"These ideas or objects of sense are commonly supposed to be pictures or representations of things without us . . . and the truth or reality of them is conceived to consist in their being exact pictures of things or objects without us, which are supposed to be the real things. But as it is impossible for us to perceive what is without our minds, and consequently, what those supposed originals are, and whether these ideas of ours are just resemblances of them or not; I am afraid this notion of them will lead us into an inextricable scepticism. I am therefore apt to think that these ideas, or immediate objects of sense, are the real things . . . and that the reality of them consists in their stability and consistence, or their being, in a stable manner, exhibited to our minds, or produced in them, and in a steady connection with each other, conformable to certain fixed laws of nature, which the great Father of Spirits hath established to

Himself, according to which He constantly operates and affects our minds, and from which He will not vary, unless upon extraordinary occasions, as in the case of miracles." (pp. 375-6.)

The Principles of Aesthetics, as Johnson saw them, are ably stated in the 16th Section of the Second Chapter of the Noetica (Schneider, II, pp. 392-3), and Ethics receives an able exposition in Part Two of the Elements (*ibid.*, pp. 442-518). While Religion is not treated in this work, it receives ample consideration in Johnson's Sermons and other writings.

"The religious obligation we are under to those actions and forbearances that are necessary to our happiness in the whole, is the consideration that they are the will and law of God, our Creator, Preserver, and supreme moral Governor, the great Author, Head and Lord of the whole social system, enforced by the sanctions of eternal rewards and punishments, to whom we are justly accountable for all our behavior, and by whom we must expect to be treated well or ill, according as that shall be found to be good or bad." [43]

IX. *Sleep, Trance and Pathology*

Sleep and Trance are not considered in the Elements, and Pathology is only hinted at in one connection ("supposing our organs rightly disposed and situated"). America had to wait for Smith, Rush and Upham for an interest in abnormal psychology.

X. *Genetic, Individual, and Social Psychology*

In this field Samuel Johnson was astonishingly original, deriving possibly from Locke an interest in the origins of mental processes, but exceeding the Englishman in his treatment of the subject.

"Mean time, I would, in pursuance of my first design, make a few observations, agreeable to the sketch here laid down, on the gradual progress of the human mind, from the first notices of sense and intellect, to its highest perfection and happiness. And as to its first notices, they are doubtless those of sense, but directly joined with a consciousness of its perfections. Warmth and hunger, and probably some pains, are, perhaps, all the sensations it hath before its birth; and when it comes into the light of this world, it is directly impressed with the sense of light and colors, as well as sounds, tastes, odors, and frequent uneasy and painful sensations, etc., all which still more and more awaken the consciousness; and every fresh notice of sense and consciousness, still goes on to excite its admiration, and engage its attention. And being a perfect stranger to everything about it, it hath every thing to learn; to which it diligently applies itself, as its consciousness more and more awakens, upon the repetition, every moment, of fresh impressions of sense; till, by degrees, having a great number of feelings, tastes, odors, sounds and visible objects, frequently repeating their several impressions, its conscious memory still enlarging, it begins, by means of the intellectual light, with which it finds its consciousness attended, gradually to collect and re-collect the several relations and connections it observes to obtain among its various ideas. And at length, when it is in ease, it discovereth a wonderful curiosity and delight in observing these connections, as well as being impressed with new ideas." (pp. 422-3.)

This interest in *genetic psychology* is pursued through fourteen fascinating pages of the Elements, with amazing acuteness and an extraordinary anticipation of modern pedagogical principles and devices.[44] In an age in which Jonathan Edwards referred to children as "little vipers," Johnson writes:

"It seems evident that those little creatures, from the beginning do consider, reflect and think a prodigious deal more than we are commonly apt to imagine. . . We ought to think little children to be persons of much more importance than we usually apprehend them to be; and how indulgent we should be to their inquisitive curiosity as being strangers; with how much candor, patience and care, we ought to bear with them and instruct them; with how much decency, honor and integrity, we ought to treat them; and how careful it concerns us to be, not to say or do anything to them, or before them, that savors of falsehood or deceit, or that is in any kind indecent or vicious. Pueris maxima debetur reverentia is a good trite old saying." (pp. 423-4.)

Jones sums up Johnson's chief pedagogical principles thus:

"Proceed from the general to the particular; from the concrete to the abstract; respect the personality of the child; make his work pleasant for him if possible, and give primary emphasis to the development of the moral side of his character." [45]

Johnson displays an interest also in what is now called *comparative* or *animal psychology*.

"[Animals] appear to see, hear, etc. and to feel pleasure and pain as I do, and can move themselves spontaneously from place to place; yet they have but low, groveling sensations, exertions and enjoyments. They appear to have no notion of any kind but the objects of sense, can conceive nothing of duty and sin, and seem capable of no enjoyment of any thing but meat and drink, and the means of continuing their species, and defending themselves; and these only are the things to which their exertions and activity tend.

"With regard to these, they have, indeed, a wonderful sagacity, and what looks like reasoning, design and contrivance, and a social tendency; but these do not seem to be any thing of their own, because they have them originally, and do not acquire them by teaching, trial and industry. This sagacity therefore seems to be what we call an instinct; by which word, nothing else can be meant, but that they are rather passively acted and conducted by some other being; some governing mind on whom they depend, according to certain laws of nature which He hath established, than that they act from any principle of deliberation and design within themselves." (pp. 454-5.)

Individual psychology is still in the future, though it is easy to find statements from Plato on that show that philosophers of all ages were keenly aware of the innate and acquired differences in individuals. *Social psychology* too is a development of the twentieth century, although Aristotle had written that man is a "political animal," and Johnson shows a leaning toward considerations that, fully developed, were to shape up into the new science. For example, he writes:

"As to those of my own species (from which by analogy I may form some notion of them) I find we were evidently made for society, being furnished with the power of speech as well as reason, whereby we are capable of entering into the understanding of each other's minds and sentiments, and of holding mutual intercourse and conversation one with another, and jointly conspiring to promote our common well-being." [46]

This is a fair sample of the early American psychology. It was published in 1752 in the first American text in Philosophy, and there is nothing superior to it on the other side of the Atlantic. In grasp and penetration it ranks with the best work of Hobbes, Locke, Berkeley and Hume, of

Leibniz and Wolff, and of Buffier and Condillac, as far as their psychology is concerned. While many of its sources are borrowed, much of the treatment and many elements of the content are profoundly original.

d. *Jonathan Edwards*,[47] *1703-1758*

The old Calvinism in New England was giving way to Arminianism, Deism, and Rationalism. As Parrington puts it,[48]

"The fundamental dogma of Arminianism was the doctrine of the *freedom of the will*—that the elect of God are not pre-chosen, but a righteous life and good works will bring men into the way of salvation. . . The crux of the question, it came finally to be seen by the apologists of the old order, lay in the fundamental problem of determinism. Was the will of man effectively free, or was it held in strict subjection to the stable will of God? According as the decision went touching this question, would stand or fall the entire metaphysical structure of Calvinism. To this problem [49] therefore, the best minds among the ministers directed their thought; and the historical position of *Jonathan Edwards*, greatest of the defenders of Calvinism, is revealed in its true perspective when his labors are studied in the light of this vital question."

Edwards' position in his main work, "A Careful and Strict Enquiry into the Modern Prevailing Notions of that Freedom of the Will, which is Supposed to be Essential to Moral Agency, Virtue and Vice, Reward and Punishment, Praise and Blame," is based upon three lines of argument, psychological, metaphysical, and theological. We shall be concerned only with the first of these.[50]

Edwards follows the scholastic division of the operations of the mind into cognitive and appetent.[51]

"God has endued the soul with two faculties: one is that by which it is capable of perception and speculation, or by which it discerns, and views, and judges of things; which is called the *understanding*. The other faculty is that by which the soul does not merely perceive and view things, but is in some way inclined with respect to the things it views or considers; either is inclined to them, or is disinclined or averse from them. This faculty is called by various names: it is sometimes called inclination; and as it has respect to the actions that are determined or governed by it, it is called *will*. The will and the affections of the soul are not two faculties; the affections are not essentially different from the will, nor do they differ from the mere actings of the will and inclination of the soul, but differ only in the liveliness and sensibleness of exercise. . . I humbly conceive, that the affections of the soul are not properly distinguishable from the will; as though they were two faculties of soul." [52]

Henry P. Tappan in an able analysis of Edwards sums up as follows:

"There are two cardinal faculties of the mind. (1) The intellectual—called reason or understanding. (2) The active and feeling—called will or affections. . . The first perceives and knows objects in their qualities, circumstances, and relations. The second experiences emotions and passions, or desires and choices, in relation to the objects perceived." [53]

"The *Will* is that by which the mind chooses anything. . . The faculty of the Will is that faculty or power or principle of mind by which it is capable of choosing; an act of the Will is the same as an act of choosing or choice. . . In every act of refusal, the mind chooses the absence of the thing refused." [54]

Will and desire are identical.

"I do not suppose that *Will* and *Desire* are words of precisely the same signification; Will seems to be a word of more general signification, extending to things present and absent. Desire respects something absent. . . But yet I cannot think they are so entirely distinct that they can ever be said to run counter. A man never, in any instance, wills anything contrary to his desires, or desires anything contrary to his will. . . The thing which he wills, the very same he desires; and he does not will a thing and desire the contrary in any particular.[55]

"The Will is said to be determined, when, in consequence of some action or influence, its choice is directed to, and fixed upon a particular object. . . If the Will be determined, there is a determiner. . . With respect to that grand inquiry, What determines the Will? . . . it is sufficient to my present purpose to say, it is that *motive*, which, as it stands in view of the mind, is the strongest, that determines the Will. . . Whatever is perceived or apprehended by an intelligent and voluntary agent, which has the nature and influence of a motive to volition or choice, is considered or viewed as good. (I use the term good; namely, as of the same import as agreeable). . . If the acts of the Will are excited by motives, those motives are the causes of those acts of the Will; which makes the acts of the Will necessary; as effects necessarily follow the efficiency of the cause. . . *The Will always is as the greatest apparent good is.*" [56]

A man wills what he most desires; he is free to do what he pleases, but he is not free to please what he pleases. This is the upshot of the whole argument, based psychologically on the identification of the will with the inclinations. There was no escape from the conclusion. The only hope lay in a new distribution of the faculties, separating the will from the emotions, so that the former might be under control, even though the latter were not. This new division was made by Kant in Germany,[57] and independently by Asa Burton in America, and popularized here by Thomas Upham, enabling Henry P. Tappan to meet Edwards' psychological argument with a new doctrine of the Will, based on an appeal to Consciousness.

In general Edwards drew his psychology from Locke.[58] He did not hesitate to differ from the Englishman, however, when his keen logical sense assured him that some of the positions were untenable.[59] In certain cases he reached independently conclusions drawn by Berkeley and Hume from the premises of Locke.[60] During the religious excitement of the Great Awakening he anticipated William James by making a psychological study of varieties of religious experience.[61]

His influence was great along theological lines, and his reputation as a metaphysician reached across the Atlantic. In psychology he illustrates the conclusions a rigorous logic can reach from data supplied by imperfect observation and inadequate analysis. His own country was to provide the very observation and analysis that would rectify the data and permit other equally logical but more reasonable conclusions.

e. *Thomas Clap*,[62] *1703-1767*

In 1765 Thomas Clap, who was on the point of resigning the Presidency of Yale College, after an active and stormy term of twenty-five years, published "An Essay on the Nature and Foundation of Moral Virtue and Obligation, Being a Short Introduction to the Study of Ethics." [63] It is a little tract of 66 pages, written "for the use of the Students of Yale-College," and designed to "settle the Nature of moral Virtue and Obligation upon its just and true Foundation."

The author outlines his Essay on page three:

"First, I shall consider the Nature and Standard of Moral Virtue. Secondly, The Obligation, which every moral Agent is under, to be conformed to that Standard. Thirdly, the Way whereby we may come to the Knowledge of that Standard, and of such a Temper and Conduct as is a Conformity to it. Lastly, I shall exhibit a brief and general Scheme of moral Virtues and Duties."

The standard proposed is conformity to the moral perfections of God. The obligation to conform arises principally from the infinite and absolute perfection of the divine nature. Divine revelation is the only way and means whereby we can know what the perfections of God are and what dispositions and conduct in us is a conformity to them. Duties are classified into three groups: to God, to our neighbors, and to ourselves.

"This is a short and general Scheme of all the Duties incumbent upon Men, together with the Foundation of the Obligation they are under to perform them. Upon these Principles a Man may safely and profitably read the common Systems of Ethics; which, though they are generally built upon wrong Foundations, yet the external Rules of Practice are generally right and good."

The systems that Clap considers to be "built on wrong Foundations" are described and confuted.[64] In criticizing these systems the author enunciates certain psychological principles, none of which vary significantly from those of Locke and Johnson already discussed. For example,

"Now I concede that God has implanted a Principle of Self-love and Self-preservation in all Animals; and that all Brutes and the greater Part of Mankind are in fact governed by that alone. And it is an Instance of the Wisdom of God, in his providential Government of the World, that, since the greater Part of Mankind, in this fallen State, are destitute of any higher or better Principle, he has implanted this, which keeps the World in some good Order and Regulation. (p. 15.)

"Reason, considered as a Power or Faculty in Man, though it is a very great and noble Endowment, vastly superior to the brutal Instinct, yet it is subject to many Imperfections and Limitations, and in this fallen State, to many Delusions and pernicious Errors. And this arises partly from wrong Conceptions of the Objects, and partly from wrong Deductions from our own Conceptions. (p. 27.)

"By a Course of reasoning and judging upon any Law or Rule, we acquire a Habit of judging on a sudden, in particular Cases, without distinctly recollecting the Principles or Reasons upon which we formerly judged. If this be all is meant by moral Sense, Taste or Instinct, it may be conceded." (pp. 40-41.)

Brattle, Johnson, Edwards, and Clap sum up American philosophy in the eighteenth century prior to the Revolution, as far as it reached the public in printed form. Brattle's work in logic merged into that of Levi Hedge through Isaac Watts. Johnson's text was used at King's and in Philadelphia, but had very little effect on either institution.[65] As Benjamin Franklin wrote, "Those parts [of the Elements of Philosophy] that savor of what is called Berkeleyism, are not well understood here." [66]

Edwards' position on determinism called forth a storm of controversy which raged until Tappan and Hazard gave it the coup de grâce, and the spell "with which the Freedom of the Will was invested by an almost sacred tradition" [67] was broken. Clap was destined to repose peacefully in brief summaries of early American philosophies. But a new gospel had already arisen in Scotland.

The year before the publication of Clap's Ethics,

Thomas Reid had given the world his Enquiry into the Human Mind. His John the Baptist arrived in America in 1768 in the person of the new President of Princeton. The Scottish Philosophy was destined to sweep everything before it.

CHAPTER TWO

THE PERIOD OF INTELLECTUAL PHILOSOPHY

The Scottish Philosophy, 1776-1827

IN the second period of the development of psychology in America, from the Revolution to the Civil War, the Scottish Philosophy was supreme, the dividing point in 1827 merely representing a shift from the original texts of Reid, Stewart and Brown to the embodiments of their points of view in products of American. McCosh gives three characteristics of the Scottish school, the protest of an outraged Presbyterianism to the conclusions of Berkeley and Hume: "1. It proceeds on the method of observation. . . . 2. It employs self-consciousness as the instrument of observation . . . and 3. By the observations of consciousness, principles are reached which are prior to and independent of experience." [1]

The latter part of the period was also influenced by the work of Hamilton, Cousin, and, to a lesser extent, of Kant. British phrenology, French abnormal psychology, and German anthropology wielded a certain influence, but the British association psychology and the German physiology and psycho-physics, while chronologically within this period, made themselves felt in America after the Civil War, and will be considered in the next section.

During the period, the population increased tenfold, moved westward, and changed radically in ethnic stock and cultural outlook. The Revolution had involved the whole country and left it completely demoralized, but after the recovery there ensued years of unprecedented commercial development. The social life of the intelligentsia was profoundly altered by new contacts with the Old World, particularly with France.

"From 1789 to 1805, deism assailed more vigorously than ever before the supernatural revelation of Christianity." [2]

"The breakdown of the old religion to some extent, and the narrowness of emotionally starved lives, provided a hotbed for the rapid spread of new religious ideas no matter how crude." [3]

With the coming of a new wave of immigration, communicants of the Roman Catholic faith also increased in number.

"The effect of the War for Independence on all types of schools was disastrous," [4] but between 1820 and the Civil War, great educational progress was made, and "Every essential feature of modern public education was either worked out or fairly anticipated in the United States by the middle of the century." [5]

The tendency to establish higher schools with a more practical content than that of the Latin Grammar School resulted in the transition academy, where among the new subjects taught was Intellectual Philosophy.[6] Here in the general exuberance of this prolific period we find psychology emerging from its ancient halls and reaching a larger class of students. Some of the psychology texts of this time were designed for these new schools, and particularly for the "female academies," of which there were a great number.

The college emerged from the War shattered and disorganized. Between 1790 and 1800 Harvard graduated fewer students than it had during the years of the War itself. After the Dartmouth College case, however, there began a great period of private and denominational effort, and the number of colleges increased from 9 before the Revolution to 150 by the middle of the century. The colleges varied in size and equipment, but were remarkably alike in aims and methods.[7] The Report of the Yale Faculty in 1827[8] stamped the curriculum with an unimpeachable authority, and fixed it definitely for the balance of the period. Education was discipline, and the study of the classics was the proper training of the mental faculties. The Professor of Moral Philosophy taught Rhetoric and Criticism in the Sophomore year, Logic, Moral Philosophy and Natural Theology to the Juniors, and Natural and Political Law and Metaphysics to the Seniors.[9] Reid, Stewart, Beattie, and Brown were the regular texts in Intellectual Philosophy, supplanted or supplemented after 1827 by American adaptations.[10]

AMERICAN PSYCHOLOGY

American scholarship rests upon the work of *J. D. Gros* at Columbia, *John Witherspoon* and *S. Stanhope Smith* at Princeton, *Levi Hedge* at Harvard, *Frederick Beasley* and *Benjamin Rush* at Philadelphia, and an "obscure Vermont preacher," *Asa Burton,* who wrote "one of the classics of New England theology, and one of the great influential books of the world."[11] Gros has given us a classic statement of scholastic psychology, Witherspoon and Smith fastened the Scottish philosophy upon the College of New Jersey, dealing a death blow to the Idealism they found there, Hedge amplified the psychological content of Logic in the tradition of Brattle, Beasley undertook a vindication of John Locke, and Rush established abnormal psychology in America. Burton framed the argument by which the psychological fallacy of Jonathan Edwards could be refuted in psychological terms by H. P. Tappan.

a. *Johann Daniel Gros*,[12] *1738-1812*

J. D. Gros, a "Minister of the German Reformed Church in the City of New York, and Professor of Moral Philosophy, Geography and Chronology in Columbia College," [13] published in 1795 a text entitled

"Natural Principles of RECTITUDE, for the Conduct of Man in all States and Situations of Life, demonstrated and explained in a Systematic Treatise on Moral Philosophy, comprehending the Law of Nature, Ethics, Natural Jurisprudence, General Oeconomy, Politics, and the law of Nations.

"Omnes Indiae opes superat mens conscii recti" [14]

The treatise is developed *more geometrico* in the style of Spinoza. After a series of preliminary definitions we are informed that

MORAL PHILOSOPHY

"Is that science which gives rules for the direction of the will of man in his moral state, or in his pursuit after happiness.

"This science is generally divided into three parts:

"The first contains the law of nature. . . The second shows how those principles are to be applied to the various states of man. The third exhibits the application of these natural principles to the states of the nations of the earth.

THE LAW OF NATURE

"Is that science which treats of the natural and invariable principles of justice and equity, by which human conduct ought to be regulated.

"It contains five chapters: The first treats of human actions in general, and particularly their morality or immorality. The second, of moral obligation. The third, of natural law. The fourth, of the different degrees of morality or immorality. The fifth, of moral imputation." (pp. 10-11.)

Man is a living creature, endowed with an *organic body*, and a *rational soul*.[15] Soul is defined to be a power susceptible and capable of representations. The different modes in which that power exerts itself are termed *faculties*.

"Living creatures endowed with an organic body and a soul, are called animals. Man differs from other animals principally in this, that his soul is rational; according to his animal nature, he has numberless determinations in common with brutes. . . There is the strictest harmony between the sensations of our mind and the mutations excited in our organs. By this indissoluble union and harmony, soul and body constitute one suppositum, that is, a complete incommunicable substance. If such a suppositum is intelligent, it constitutes a physical person.

"All mutations flowing from the mechanisms of the body and the natural frame of the mind, in certain respects, are hypothetically natural; for in divers persons they are different, nay, very often in the same individual. This difference is most probably in consequence of their originating from different sources, some originating in the soul, others resulting from the body. The mind is not always equally vigilant, the body may be deranged; the state of childhood differs from that of manhood, that of sickness from a state of health. Whatever may be the origin or the qualifying causes of those different mutations, so much is certain, that they affect the whole man, and modify his physical state, that he becomes an individual person, distinct from all others in constitution, complexion, disposition, etc. Natural mutations do not interest the moralist any farther than as they affect or are affected by spontaneity, inclination and will. . ."

The following is Gros' distribution of the faculties, following Thomas Aquinas: [16]

I. *Cognoscitive*
  1. *Inferior* (by which we have representations of material objects)
      (1) *Sensation* (that faculty by which we have representations of material objects present)
      (2) *Imagination* (by which we have representations of material objects absent, but which have once been wholly present)
      (3) *Fancy* (by which we form representations of such absent material objects as have once been present in part)
  2. *Superior* (by which we are enabled to form representations of immaterial objects)
      (1) *Attention* (the faculty of continuing our thoughts)
      (2) *Reflection* (the faculty of continuing attention)
      (3) *Understanding* (the faculty of forming distinct ideas of things)
      (4) *Reason* (the faculty of seeing the connection of things in particular)
      (5) *Judgment* (the faculty of comparing ideas)

II. *Appetitive* (that faculty by which we feel an appetite for things represented as good, and are averse to those which are represented as bad)
  1. *Inferior—Passions* (strong and predominant appetites or aversions)
      (1) Agreeable (having good for their object)
          a. Based on *pleasure* (arising from a strong representation of a good in our possession)

      b. Based on *desire* (when there is a great probability of obtaining a good yet in expectation)

  (2) Disagreeable (having evil for their object)

      a. Based on *pain* (caused by the representation that we labor under the pressure of a present evil)

      b. Based on *fear* (arising from the thought that an evil hangs over our head)

  2. *Superior—Will* (rational appetite and aversion, when our mind is actuated by representations of our understanding)

The acts of the will are *volition* and *nolition*. In the exercise of these acts, we may distinguish the following operations of the mind:

  (1) A distinct idea of an object is formed

  (2) Consequences must be attended to . . .

  (3) The object with those consequences is referred to our state, and a conclusion formed.

"Hence it is evident, that the acts of the will cannot be exercised without the exercise of attention, reflection, understanding, reason, and judgment.

"Appetite and aversion caused by sensation, imagination or fancy constitute the inferior appetitive faculty; but if they take rise in consequence of acts of the understanding, they must be considered as exertions of the superior; they are acts of the will. Appetite and aversion follow certain laws; for they are indissolubly connected with the representations of good and evil. . . Appetites and aversions change with our representations; the boy ceases to dislike the school if he can be made to see the evil of idleness.

"All other passions, distinguished in language by different names, are not affections different in their nature, but only degrees either of pleasure or desire, or pain or fear; as joy, anxiety, despair, terror, mortification, etc. An habitual indulgence of sense and passion plunges us into sensuality and causes propensity. A kind of appetite and aversion, not founded upon representations of the mind, is called instinct, as hunger, thirst, etc.

"Experience evinces, that brutes, in conformity to their sensitive representations, also have their sensitive appetite and aversion, exercise indifference, are actuated by propensities and by instinct. It is likewise evident from common observation, that their appetites and aversions are generally more confined and infinitely better directed than those of man; their passions and propensities are but of the one or the other kind, and their vehemency keeps pace with an irritating cause, or corresponds with the destiny, defence, or support of their existence. Everything indicates that sense and instinct are given them for their guide; everything manifests infinite power, wisdom and goodness in him who made them.

"But it is not so with man; he is prone to sensuality; various passions obscure and disturb his mind, plunge him into error, sin and misery: sense, passions, instinct, therefore, cannot have been designed by the wise Creator to be the directors of the ways of man.

"What great cause is there to bless God that he has given him another, a better guide; that he hath clothed human nature with a dignity superior to all creatures here on earth; that he has created his soul a spirit? Man is not to follow sense, but as it is directed by understanding and reason; these are to direct the steps of his feet, the desires of his heart—not to obey but to regulate sense and passion."

This systematic, scholarly exposition of the scholastic philosophy should be compared with the pathetic synopsis in the youthful Notebook of Samuel Johnson. It was the last word of a thorough German in a language that was already dead except in the conservative Catholic schools.[17]

Gros was a man of personal charm, beloved by his students,[18] but his psychology was destined to bow before the onslaught of Scottish Realism.

b. *John Witherspoon* [19] *(1722-1794) and S. Stanhope Smith (1750-1819)*

John Witherspoon is important in the history of American psychology as the man who first introduced the Scottish philosophy to America.

"[He] had the distinction of being the first college head in the country to set forth in his classroom a definite system of ethics. This system, as Lansing Collins . . . has said, was the realism of Thomas Reid and the Scottish common sense school." [20]

"Introduced into Princeton by Witherspoon, this Scottish philosophy of common sense displaced the idealistic tendencies in vogue there, . . . came to dominate Princeton, and through Princeton the Presbyterian institutions of the West and South that grew up under its influence. Even in the New England colleges the Scottish realism gained ground." [21]

Witherspoon's psychology is contained in the first three of his sixteen Lectures on Moral Philosophy, delivered at the College of New Jersey between 1768 and 1794, and first printed in his Complete Works in 1800.[22]

"The Doctor's Lectures on morals, notwithstanding they assume the form of regular discourses, were in fact, viewed by himself as little more than a syllabus or compend, on which he might enlarge before a class at times of recitation . . . he did not intend these lectures for the press." [23]

He thus states the principles of the Scotch school:

"That our senses are to be trusted in the information they give us, seems to me a first principle, because they are the foundation of all our reasonings. The few exceptions of accidental irregularities in the senses, can found no just objection to this, as there are too many plain and obvious ways of discovering and correcting it. . . Some late writers have advanced the great apparent reason, that there are certain first principles or *dictates of common sense* [24] which are either simple perceptions, or seen with intuitive evidence. These are the foundation of all reasoning, and without these, to reason is a word without a meaning. They can no more be proved than you can prove an axiom in mathematical science. These authors of Scotland [25] have lately produced and supported this opinion, to resolve at once all the refinements and metaphysical objections of some infidel writers." (pp. 278, 297.)

Apart from this formal announcement of the new philosophy, Witherspoon adds very little to the body of psychological doctrine already developed. He makes some shrewd comments on philosophical method, emphasizes the relation of ethics and psychology, discusses the relation of soul and body, and suggests a threefold division of the mental faculties.

"Moral Philosophy is that branch of Science which treats of the principles and laws of Duty or Morals. It is called Philosophy, because it is an inquiry into the nature and grounds of moral obligation by reason, as distinct from revelation. Hence arises a question, is it lawful, and is it safe or useful to separate moral philosophy from religion? . . . If the Scripture is true, the discoveries of reason cannot be contrary to it; and therefore it has nothing to fear from that quarter. And as we are certain it can do no evil, so there is a probability that it may do some good. . . The noble and eminent improvements in natural philosophy, which have been made since the end of the last century, have been far from hurting the interest of religion; on the contrary, they have greatly promoted it. Why should it not be the same with moral philosophy, which is indeed nothing but the knowledge of human nature?" (pp. 269-70.)

The principles of duty and obligation must be drawn from the nature of man.

"Man . . . is a compound of body and spirit. . . The body and spirit have a great reciprocal influence one upon another. The body on the temper and disposition of the soul, and the soul on the state and habit of the body. . . There are great and essential differences between man and man, as to the spirit and its proper powers. . . Such are the laws of union between the body and spirit, that many faculties are weakened and some rendered incapable of exercise, merely by an alteration of the state of the body. Memory is frequently lost and judgment weakened by old age and disease. Sometimes by a confusion of the brain in a fall the judgment is wholly disordered. The instinctive appetites of hunger, and thirst, seem to reside directly in the body. . . Some passions, particularly fear and rage, seem also to have their seat in the body, immediately producing a certain modification of the blood and spirits. . . Those that depend most upon the body are fear, anger, voluptuousness, and those that depend least upon it, are ambition, envy, covetousness." (pp. 274-5.)

"The faculties of the mind are commonly divided into these three kinds, the understanding, the will, and the affections; though perhaps it is proper to observe, that these are not three qualities wholly distinct, but different ways of exerting the same principle. It is the soul or mind that understands, wills, or is affected with pleasure and pain." [26]

His treatment of the passions is more elaborate than that of Johnson, and like a true Scotchman he shows a great interest in aesthetics.[27] He gave the coup de grâce to Berkeleyan Idealism:

"The truth is, the immaterial system, is a wild and ridiculous attempt to unsettle the principles of common sense by metaphysical reasoning, which can hardly produce any thing but contempt in the generality of persons who hear it, and which I verily believe, never produced conviction even on the persons who pretend to espouse it." [28]

The task of filling in the outlines of his psychology, however, he left to his son-in-law, Stanhope Smith.

Samuel Stanhope Smith [29] had a checkered philosophical career.

"During his collegiate course, Mr. Smith was in great danger of making shipwreck of his religious principles, in consequence of his intimacy with Mr. Periam, the Senior Tutor, who had embraced Bishop Berkeley's theory, denying the existence of the material universe. Mr. P. had so much influence over his pupil, that, for a time, he succeeded in making him not only a convert to his strange opinions, but an earnest advocate of them; insomuch that Mr. Smith's friends began to have the most serious apprehensions that he had become a permanent victim to one of the worst kinds of philosophical insanity. Happily, however, when Dr. Witherspoon arrived from Scotland, he brought with him the works of several distinguished Scottish philosophical writers, particularly Reid and Beattie, the influence of which was quickly perceptible, in bringing back this gifted young man into the regions of common sense. It was only for a short time that this aberration continued, and when his mind had become steadfast in the right, it became so for life." [30]

He was called back in 1779 to his Alma Mater, where he had already served as Tutor for upwards of two years, became Professor of Moral Philosophy, and in 1794, at the death of Witherspoon, succeeded his father-in-law as Pres-

ident of the institution. In 1812, he published "The LEC-
TURES, Corrected and Improved, which have been delivered for a series of years in the College of New-Jersey on
the Subjects of Moral and Political Philosophy." [31] The
first of the two volumes contains his contributions to psychology.

Smith opens with a definition of Philosophy in general
and Moral Philosophy in particular, and a discussion of
the rules by which it ought to be investigated.

"PHILOSOPHY is an investigation of the constitution and laws
of nature, both in the physical and moral world, as far as the
powers of the human mind, unaided by the lights of revelation,
are competent to discover it. . . [The method is] a careful
and extensive induction of facts. (p. 9.)

"Philosophy is divided into two great branches,—the natural
and the moral. . . *Moral philosophy* is an investigation of the
constitution and laws of mind, especially as it is endowed with
the power of voluntary action, and is susceptible of the sentiments of duty and obligation. . . The science of moral philosophy begins in the study of the human mind—its sensations,
perceptions, and generally, its means of acquiring knowledge—
its sentiments, dispositions and affections, and generally, its
principles of action or enjoyment—its present state, and reactions to other beings—its future hopes and fears. . . In this investigation . . . it is necessary to follow the method of analysis, and to reason from particular facts, collected by extensive
and careful observation, to the general laws of the human
mind. (pp. 12-14.)

"No law should be admitted on hypothesis but should rest
solely on an induction of facts. . . Laws collected from an
ample and accurate induction of facts should be deemed universal, till other facts occur to invalidate, or limit the conclusions
which have been drawn from them. . . Laws founded on a

partial induction of facts should not be extended beyond the limits to which they are certainly known to apply. . . Similar appearances should, because of the uniformity of nature, be referred, as far as possible, to the same causes. . . The testimony of our senses, and of all our simple perceptions, ought to be admitted as true, and no ulterior evidence required of the reality, or of the nature of the facts which they confirm." (pp. 19-23.)

He then devotes about one hundred pages to what might be called anthropology in the spirit of the contemporary German school of Fries.

He proposes to

"take a comparative view of him [man] in relation to the other species of animals upon this earth among which he evidently holds the first rank . . . consider his prolific powers . . . view him as a social being . . . and consider his capacities for improvement." (pp. 28-29.)

He anticipates Fiske in emphasizing the importance of prolonged infancy (p. 33), presents an abridgment of his book on the Causes of the Variety in the Human Species (pp. 35-52), discusses population and social institutions (Ch. III), the implications and results of the social disposition of man (Ch. IV), and language as an important instrument of communication and improvability of man (Ch. V). He then disposes briefly of animal psychology,

"We are not sufficiently acquainted with the nature of the inferior animals to know how far they possess the powers of comparison or induction." (p. 126.)

touches upon mental hygiene,

"It is not more certain that the sound and perfect exercise of the soul depend, in a great degree, upon the healthful state of the body, than that the health of the body is reciprocally affected by the state of the mind." (p. 132.)

and states his position with reference to the Idealistic Philosophy, "the philosophic delirium of hypothesis."

Psychology is concerned with

"the means by which we become acquainted with the existence, and the nature of the things with which we are surrounded; the emotions of our minds towards them arising from their several qualities, or their adaptation to our feelings;—the classes into which they are grouped, or pictures in which they are arranged by the power of imagination for our instruction and entertainment;—the inferences which we derive for the direction of our conduct from comparing, dividing, combining them through the operations of the reasoning faculty;—the affections of the soul called up by them, which are among the principal motives of human conduct through the agency of the will, the immediate principle of action;—subject, in an accountable nature, like that of man, to that sense of morality, which, in the order of nature, is intended to govern all our conduct towards other intelligent beings. . . The powers of our nature may be comprehended under the heads of *sensation,*—of *sentiment,*—of *imagination,*—of *reasoning,*—of *volition,*—and of *the moral principle.*" (pp. 140-141.)

Sensation receives a more adequate treatment than in any of the previous American writers (pp. 168-183), the nervous system, "which may be regarded as an expansion of the brain distributed in these fine and delicate filaments to every part of the body" (p. 147), is mentioned for the first time in the history of American psychology, pathological cases are cited and notice is taken of individual differences (pp. 151-167) and the vibration theory of David Hartley receives a qualified approval (p. 147 ff.). The external senses are differentiated from the internal, which furnish the mind with three classes or modes of internal feeling: (1) Those which relate to the acts and sentiments of our own minds, (2) Those which relate to the fine arts, and (3) Those which relate to morals.

"Those physical and moral powers, or properties, which are the immediate springs and incentives of action in man" (p. 223) are taken up under eight heads:

"*Propensity* may be defined to be a natural tendency to perform certain actions, or to seek for certain enjoyments, prior to reflection, or to any experience we have had of the good or ill effects of these actions, or of those enjoyments. . . Propensities are divided into the bodily, mental, and mixed. . . The propensities which have their seat chiefly in the body, are more usually called appetites. Among the mental propensities . . . may be ranked curiosity to know, ambition to excel, the love of imitation, etc. . . The mixed propensities . . . are those which appear in the protection, caresses and love of children, in the inclination to society. . . (pp. 224-5.)

"*Instinct* is a kind of mechanical operation, producing actions relative to our preservation, or enjoyment, simply under the impulse of a strong natural feeling, in which the higher powers of the mind have not any concern. (p. 226.)

"[*Habit* is] that facility and perfection in performing an action which is the result of frequent repetition. But the ease of execution commonly produces pleasure in the performance. (p. 230.)

"*Sentiment* may be defined to be an emotion of the mind relative to good or evil, present or future, in ourselves or others. It produces a state of feeling rather predisposing to action in a certain direction, than exciting to any immediate effort. (pp. 232-3.)

"*Imagination* . . . is that active principle . . . defined by

Dr. Ferguson to be the faculty of creating in the mind the images of objects, or scenes which have no real existence in nature; or of representing real objects, and scenes invested with all their circumstances and qualities; those circumstances and qualities, especially which escape the notice of ordinary observers, and strike only the finer or secondary powers of sensation, such as beauty, sublimity, proportion, grace, or harmony."

The *affections* or *passions* are discussed in a lecture of some 25 pages (pp. 249-274), including an historical treatment of the subject, an analysis, and a reference to the works of Watts and Beattie as "worthy of your perusal."

The chief offices of *reason* are stated (p. 273), but the student is referred to the science of logic for adequate treatment.

"The *will* is that power of the soul, and volition the exercise of that power which is the immediate cause of action in man (p. 275). . . . The nature of the will is understood, as far as we understand any of the acts or powers of our own minds, only by consciousness (p. 276). The principal enquiry on this subject . . . relates to the freedom of the will, as it is generally expressed; or, as it ought, perhaps, to be more definitely stated, the freedom of the mind in her volitions. . . We shall arrive at clearer ideas upon this subject, and approach nearer the truth, by rejecting the phraseology of both parties, and, instead of admitting the hypotheses, either that the will determines itself, or that it is determined by the last or strongest motive, to lay it down as a principle upon this question, that the mind alone determines the acts of the will, as it does all its other operations."

Smith's conclusions may be summed up in his own words:

"In the various operations of the mind in which the influence of the will is concerned, we are usually sensible of the solicita-

tion of some motive. . . Although these motives prompt to action, and, in many cases, direct the tenor of our actions, yet do
we never perceive that they impose upon the mind any necessary constraint in acting. . . The mind has the power of beginning action, or exerting the acts of the will by its own in-
trinsic energy . . . one of the principal distinctions between
spirit and matter." (pp. 287-90.)

The Lectures close with a discussion of the *Moral
Faculty*.

"The moral faculty, or, as Dr. Hutcheson, and Lord Shaftesbury, have denominated it, the moral sense . . . is that principle whence alone we derive the conceptions of duty and obligation, and of right and wrong applied to human dispositions
and conduct. . . This sense is as much the natural and the
only organ (if that term may be applied to any of our principles
of internal sensation) of the ideas of duty and of right, and
their contraries, as the eye is of those of color, or the ear of
sound." [32]

Although it is included in a comprehensive course in
Moral Philosophy, which involves "material from the
fields of biology and psychology, of politics and economics,
as well as of religion and ethics," [33] we have at last an extensive manual of psychology, abreast of the latest developments in the field, most sympathetic to the inductive
method, and singularly full of promise for the future.

c. *Levi Hedge,*[34] *1766-1844*

In 1819 Levi Hedge published the "Elements of
Logick, or a Summary of the General Principles and Different Modes of Reasoning," "to furnish rules for the
direction of the understanding in its various inquiries after

knowledge." Part First is a "Description of the leading Affections and Operations of the Mind." [35]

"The purpose of Logic is to direct the intellectual powers in the investigation of truth, and in the communication of it to others. Its foundation is laid in the philosophy of the human mind. . . The powers of the mind, like those of the body, must be strengthened by use. (pp. 13-14.)

"*Perception* is the first state of affection of the human mind. The instruments of perception are the five corporeal senses. . . From experience we learn, that a sensible alteration takes place in the mind, whenever any outward object is so situated, as to affect any of the senses. The change, produced in the mind by the impression of the object on the organ of sense, is denominated *sensation*. The word *perception* denotes the knowledge, that we gain by sensation, of some quality in the object; which knowledge may be retained by the mind after the object is removed, and it is then usually called an *idea* or *notion*. . .

"*Consciousness,* or reflection, is that notice, which the mind takes of its own operations, and modes of existence. . . By consciousness, we learn what is expressed by the words compare, reason, doubt, assent, joy in the same manner as, by perception, we gain a knowledge of sweet, green, soft, cold. Both perception and consciousness, considered apart from any acts of attention, accompanying them, are involuntary states of mind. We are often active in bringing external objects within our view, and in varying their position, for the purpose of careful consideration; so, by a voluntary effort, we excite operations, and cause changes in the mind; but the knowledge, that we gain in each case, of the subjects thus presented, is without any act of the will. (pp. 15-18.)

"*Attention* expresses the immediate direction of the mind to a subject. . . Attention is considered a voluntary act of the mind, but it is not at all times equally subject to our command,

and in young children is wholly involuntary. . . Attention is
. . . essential to memory. (pp. 19-21.)

"When the mind contemplates two things in reference to
each other, it performs the operation of comparing." (p. iv.)

"*Abstraction* literally implies the separation of one thing from
another; but, as a mental operation, it denotes only a partial
consideration of any thing. It is the act of considering one or
more of the properties or circumstances of an object, apart from
the rest. . . As the quality, thus mentally separated from those
existing with it, may be found in numerous subjects, the name
applied to it becomes a general term. . . This power . . . is
the foundation of all classification, and gives rise to the general
words of language. (pp. 23-25.)

"By the *association of ideas* it is understood that connection
among the thoughts, affections, and operations of the mind, by
which one has a tendency to introduce another. . . The following are among the most obvious of the principles of association:
resemblance or analogy, opposition or contrast, contiguity or
nearness of time and place, and cause and effect, premises and
consequences. . . The same circumstances may suggest different trains of thought to different persons, and to the same person at different times. (pp. 25-28.)

"To *analyze* is nothing more, than to distinguish successively
the several parts of any compound subject."

Direct citation and footnote references indicate Reid's
Essays, Stewart's Elements and Beattie's Dissertations as
principal sources of the psychology. Hedge's text was well-
written, became instantly popular, and, long used as a manual of logic, aided in keeping the principles of the Scottish
philosophy before the minds of the college students.

d. *Benjamin Rush* [36] *(1745-1813) and Frederick Beasley (1777-1845)*

The scene in Pennsylvania is enlivened by the activity and writings of two influential men, Benjamin Rush, physician, patriot, and philosopher, and Frederick Beasley, Provost of the University of Pennsylvania from 1813 to 1828, and ardent defender of John Locke against the libels and misinterpretations of the Scottish School.

Rush is deserving of a whole volume rather than a part of a section.

"He was a great physician, a talented teacher, a competent scientist, an able organizer, a felicitous writer, a vigorous social reformer, an earnest philanthropist, a creative scholar, and a devoted patriot." [37]

"His name was familiar to the medical world as the Sydenham of America. His accurate observations and correct discrimination of epidemic diseases well entitled him to this distinction; while in the original energy of his reasoning he far excelled his prototype." [38]

Allibone lists 25 topics treated in his various pamphlets, including Education, Insanity, and Mental and Moral Philosophy.[39] Riley calls him the "father of psychiatry in America . . . for his whole life was filled with speculations as to the practical application of mental medicine." [40] His most definite contributions to psychology are contained in the Fourth of his Sixteen Introductory Lectures to his Course on the Institutes and Practice of Medicine,[41] five of the Chapters in the First Volume of Medical Inquiries and Observations,[42] and in a special Volume on the Diseases of the Mind.[43]

Dr. Rush enumerates the faculties and operations of the mind.

"Its *faculties* are, understanding, memory, imagination, passions, the principle of faith, will, the moral faculty, conscience, and the sense of Deity. Its principal *operations,* after sensation, are perception, association, judgment, reasoning and volition. All its subordinate operations, which are known by the names of attention, reflection, contemplation, wit, consciousness, and the like, are nothing but modifications of the five principal operations that have been mentioned." [44]

"All the operations in the mind are the effects of motions previously excited in the brain, and every idea and thought appears to depend upon a motion peculiar to itself. In a sound state of the mind these motions are regular, and succeed impressions upon the brain with the same certainty and uniformity that perceptions succeed impressions upon the senses in their sound state."

In a Lecture on the Influence of Physical Causes in Promoting an Increase of the Strength and Activity of the Intellectual Faculties of Man, he discusses the agents which improve the understanding, the memory, and the imagination. He devotes a special Lecture to an Inquiry into the Influence of Physical Causes upon the Moral Faculty.[45] The causes which lessen the quantity of mind are taken up in the Volume on the Diseases of the Mind, which treats systematically of derangements of the understanding, the will, the believing faculty, the memory, the passions, and the moral faculty, with fruitful digressions into the subject of dreams and illusions.

Rush ventures to coin the word "phrenology" to designate the science of the mind.[46] He stresses the utility of a knowledge of the faculties and operations of the mind, and the value of mental hygiene.

"Man is said to be a compound of soul and body. However proper this language may be in religion, it is not so in medicine. He is, in the eye of a physician, a single and indivisible being, for so intimately united are his soul and body, that one cannot be moved, without the other. The actions of the former upon the latter are numerous and important. They influence many of the functions of the body in health. They are the cause of many diseases; and if properly directed, they may easily be made to afford many useful remedies." [47]

He made the first systematic studies in America of abnormal mentality, and used the technique of suggestion a century before the Nancy school.

"His excursions into the almost virgin field of psychiatry were remarkable for their originality and insight." [48]

"Rush frequently asked patients to write down an account of their symptoms. They felt better for the writing and often he learned much that was enlightening about them. Was it possible that Rush, in using this procedure, called by Freud mental catharsis, anticipated the theory and practice of the psychoanalyst?" [49] Goodman.

He anticipated the Freudians in the description and even the nomenclature of phobias.[50] He was interested in dual personality,[51] and furnished the writers of psychology textbooks both in Great Britain and America for the next three generations with anecdotal material in abnormal psychology.[52]

In the year in which Rush died Frederick Beasley [53] was made Provost of the University of Pennsylvania and Professor of Moral Philosophy. Renewing his studies in the science of mind, which he had begun at Princeton under the "venerable president Smith," [54] he thought he perceived

"that the Scottish metaphysicians had either inadvertently or wilfully done their predecessors very great injustice, in their animadversions upon their writings, ascribed to them opinions which they never held, assumed to themselves the merit of broaching and promulgating the very doctrines which they taught, and, at the same time, had fallen into the grossest errors in that new system of pneumatology, which they claimed the credit of introducing. Dr. Reid, who is, undoubtedly, the greatest writer upon these topics that Scotland has produced . . . saw the absurd and preposterous conclusions of Mr. Hume, and that . . . he professes to ground them upon the principles of Mr. Locke; but he did not take the pains to ascertain, whether or not, those were the genuine doctrines of Locke. . .

"I trust I shall be able to show . . . that there is no kind of connection between the premises of Mr. Hume or Berkeley, and the principles of Mr. Locke. And, should I be so fortunate as to succeed in accomplishing this task . . . not only will Mr. Locke and other philosophers, be restored to those well-merited honours, from which, for a time, at least, they have been degraded, but no inconsiderable service will have been rendered also, to the interesting science of human nature." (pp. ii-iv.)

To accomplish this vindication of Locke, Provost Beasley wrote a volume of 561 pages, entitled "A Search for Truth in the Science of the Human Mind," Part First.[55] He concludes with these words:

"The intelligent reader will perceive that we have arrived at the conclusion of our volume, without having exhausted our subject. Many of the most interesting powers of the mind remain to be treated of, and its most interesting phenomena to be solved. The powers of abstraction, composition, imagination, reason, the will, the affections, together with all the social and moral faculties will, on a future occasion, we trust, should our life and health be continued, open to us a large and interesting field of investigation." (p. 561. Part Second was never published.)

Beasley thus defines the object of "pneumatology, or the science of the human mind":

"To trace the progress of the understanding in the acquisition of knowledge, to pursue it from its earliest beginnings in those simple perceptions to which it attains by means of the external senses and reflex acts of its own, to its most complex and sublime combinations and conclusions." (p. 17.)

After clearing the ground by a lengthy discussion of cause and effect, and pouring out his withering scorn upon "the intellectual fooleries and sceptical impieties of Mr. Hume," [56] he proceeds to the subject of perception, to which he devotes 370 pages, digressing into a treatment of dreams, illusions, and abnormal psychology, and devoting several chapters to the genetic considerations promised in the definition of pneumatology. The remaining 60 pages take a cursory view of discernment, judgment, wit, attention, intention, memory, and conception.

The good Provost was tilting at windmills, for the Scottish philosophy had come to stay. He himself, "in his eagerness to defend Locke against the charge of scepticism, comes in the end to propound an essentially realistic doctrine." [57] The new wave of Scotch-Irish immigrants "carried along with their Presbyterian connections their philosophy of common sense," [58] and Samuel Miller expressed the feeling of the academic world when he wrote in his Brief Retrospect of the Eighteenth Century that "the principles and reasonings of certain modern metaphysicians of North Britain, certainly form the most important accession which the philosophy of mind has received since the time of Mr. Locke." [59]

e. *Asa Burton,*[60] *1752-1836*

Jonathan Edwards had flung down the gauntlet to all the opponents of Calvinism by his inexorably logical demonstration that the human will is fully determined by the nature of the soul and the prescience of God. His conclusions were inevitable, but it was generally felt that there was an escape somewhere from a doctrine that outraged the common experience of every human being. It might well be that Edwards' analysis of the mind was at fault, and several thinkers proposed a discrimination between the feelings and the will, based on the evidence of consciousness. Samuel West suggested a threefold division of the faculties in his Essays on Liberty and Necessity.

"There are *three* essential *faculties* or properties of the mind, which ought always to be considered distinctly, and should never be confounded nor blended together; and these are *Perception, Propension,* and *Will.* The last only is properly the active faculty of the mind. In Perception I include apprehension, judgment, and memory; for memory is only the reviving of past perceptions, with a consciousness that we have had those perceptions before. Judgment is the perceiving of the agreement or disagreement of two or more things compared together. Apprehension is the ready and quick perception of the reality of things presented to our view." [61]

John Witherspoon had already advanced a similar division. Nathaniel W. Taylor,[62] Professor at Yale in the Department of Theology opened in 1822, Thomas C. Upham of Bowdoin College, Henry P. Tappan, then Professor in the University of the City of New York, and Asa Mahan, President of Oberlin, were all to have a hand in developing, popularizing, and utilizing this new distribution of the faculties in reply to Edwards' determinism.

The most important writer in this connection was Asa Burton, a country preacher, who in the quiet of his study, by painstaking self-analysis and persistent logic, arrived independently at a threefold division of the mental faculties, and published his findings in a book of "Essays on Some of the First Principles of Metaphysicks, Ethicks, and Theology." [63]

"The Author of the following essays, when he first entered on the study of theology, felt the importance of forming a just and true theory of the human mind. This feeling prompted him to read with attention all the most noted and distinguished authors, he could find, on the subject of pneumatology [Note; this was in 1777; Kant's Kritik was published in 1781].—He expected, by studying them, to digest a true system. This course he pursued for several years. When he had carefully attended to English, Scotch, French and German authors, instead of finding increased light, his mind was more darkened and perplexed with respect to several parts of this very important subject. Failing of success in this way, he determined to lay aside reading of authors, except occasionally, and make an attempt *by an exertion of his own powers,* to arrange his thoughts systematically on the principles and operations of the human mind. . . He determined not to adopt the plan or theory of any authors he had ever read, for this reason; he does not agree, except in part, with the system or plan of any preceding author. . . That theory of the mind, which was the result of much study . . . it is the object of these essays to illustrate and explain. . .

"It has been found by experience, that the *classing of objects* assists the memory, and renders the acquisition of knowledge more easy, and rapid. This is the plan the author designs to adopt with respect to operations of the mind. . . The operations of the mind are not all of one kind, but they differ from each other; for which reason they ought to be formed into distinct, general classes; and these general classes may be divided, according to their specific differences. *This method will give a systematic arrangement to the several divisions of mental operations.*" (pp. 3, 5.)

His book fell into the hands of Upham, who was struggling with the problem of methodology for his text on mental philosophy, and settled his difficulties. Upham's series of textbooks ran through many editions and was widely used in American colleges and academies, thus promulgating the tri-partite division years before Hamilton in Great Britain imported a similar scheme from Germany.

For Asa Burton psychology was the ancilla theologiae, but that did not prevent him from appealing to facts, experience, and common sense, nor from making keen introspections and drawing logical conclusions from them.

"These essays are designed as an introduction to divinity. The author's great object, in explaining what appears to him to be the true theory of the mind, is, to assist the student in acquiring a systematic and consistent knowledge of divinity. He does not purpose to attend to any question, or disquisitions relative to the mind, which are not necessary to answer this end. (p. 5.)

"In the essays on the mind, he means to take facts, experience, and common sense for his guides. He does not design to form a system on any other principles, than those which are self-evident, or capable of demonstration. Whatever opinions respecting the mind he may advance, which do not agree with experience, with facts, and the word of God, are to be rejected. (p. 4.)

"So in relation to the mind, when the number of faculties with which it is endued, and the operations of each faculty with the real differences between them are known, the way is then prepared to form them into general and specific classes. . . And if perceptions, sensations and affections, and volitions, include all the operations of the mind; these *three general classes* are sufficient. Form these three general classes into their specific divisions; then the work of classifying is finished, and a systematic view of the mind is formed. And this seems to be the only rational plan for accomplishing that end. (pp. 6-7.)

"To understand the operations of the mind distinctly, we must attend to them carefully, and refer each operation to its proper faculty. And though operations follow each other, and are connected in a train; yet we ought not to view all those thus connected as operations of the same faculty. But we ought to distinguish them according to their natures, and refer them to the classes and faculties to which they belong; and *not suffer ourselves to be imposed on by figures of speech.*" (p. 47.)

He disposes of metaphysical subtleties by a blunt statement of his belief in a material world.

"Different theories have been adopted and supported concerning our perceptions, thoughts, or conceptions. Some of the ancient philosophers believed, that men do not see the objects created, but their forms, which they called phantasms, or images. And modern philosophers have advanced various other theories on this subject. Of late there has been much dispute concerning the sense in which Locke used the term idea. Whether he meant the real object existing, or some image of it in the eye. Some have denied the existence of a material world; and such various opinions have given rise to scepticism, which has been carried to a great length. . . *It will be taken for granted through these essays, that a material world does exist, distinct from the mind;* and that all objects, of which we obtain a knowledge through the medium of our bodily senses, are real existences. It is objects as they exist, which we see, whether properties or modes; and not images, or representations of them." (pp. 21-22.)

A preliminary chapter is devoted to proving that there are mental faculties, and that they are properly classified into three great divisions.

"There was a time, when the word faculty was first used. It was then used to express some idea which the speaker then had. What was it? If the original meaning of the word is retained in our language, it was at first used to signify *a preparedness in the mind for certain operations.* It communicates no more than a simple idea. Hence it does not admit of a logical definition. (p. 13.)

"The word faculty is a term, which can no more be defined, than we can define the word pain. . . Will any person affirm that pain has no cause, has nothing which occasions it, when he has no consciousness or knowledge of that cause, or antecedent? No; he infers, from the pain he feels, the existence of something which produced it. And he may as safely infer the existence of faculties, from their operations or exercises. . . *By a faculty, then, I mean a preparedness, a fitness, a capacity, or an adaptation of the mind for those various operations, of which we are daily conscious.* (And here I would give notice, that I shall use the term operations in these essays, to denote all the thoughts, feelings or affections, and volitions of the mind. Every thought is an operation; every affection, and every volition, is an operation of the human mind. I shall generally use the word in this extensive sense.)

"And now the inquiry is, whether there is in the mind a faculty or preparedness for thinking, a preparedness for feeling, and a preparedness for willing; and whether there is not; and whether these faculties are antecedent to every operation of the mind, and objects of distinct consideration. . . Some arguments will now be adduced. . .

1. This distinction is so obvious to common sense, that it has been admitted by all nations, in every age of the world. . .

2. From our actions and operations we may safely infer the existence of faculties. That we think, feel, love, hate, choose and refuse, is certain. What is it, which thinks, which loves, which chooses; something or nothing? It must be one or the other. . . From our thoughts, we infer the faculty called the understanding, which thinks, or perceives objects; and from our feelings or affections, we infer a feeling faculty; and from our volitions, we infer the faculty termed the will, which chooses and rejects. And there is no way to avoid this inference, unless we say there may be operations without an operator; which is as inconsistent, as to assert there may be design without a designer.

3. If we have no faculties, mankind are not agents. Agents act or operate. But agency exists, antecedent to actions. Now if men have no faculties, what constitutes that agency which is employed in thinking and choosing, and which by its operations becomes visible? . . . If any persons wish for further proof, I refer them

4. To the word of God. . . 'Then opened he their *understanding*, that they might understand the scriptures.' . . 'A good man, out of the treasure of his *heart*, bringeth out that which is good; and an evil man, out of the evil treasure of his heart, bringeth forth that which is evil; for of the abundance of the heart his mouth speaketh.' . . 'Which were born, not of blood, nor of the will of the flesh, nor of the *will* of man, but of God.' . . Hence the scriptures teach us that the mind is created with *three distinct faculties*, whose operations are very different from

each other. Perceptions of objects are the operations of the understanding. The affections are the operations of the heart. And volitions are the operations of the will. These distinctions are founded on a real difference. . . To view the human mind as possessed, or, if any prefer it, composed of three distinct faculties, which are to be considered as existing antecedent to their operations, and to which very different operations are severally ascribed, are truths supported both by reason and scripture." (Ch. I, condensed.)

The following argument on the distinction between the feelings and the will made psychological history. It caught the attention of Professor Upham, who incorporated it into his Treatise on the Will, and used it later in his Mental Philosophy to justify his threefold division of the faculties.

"Why do not philosophers consider all the operations of the understanding, and the affections, as constituting but one general class of operations, and as belonging to one faculty? The reason is, they see no similarity between intellectual perceptions and affections. A perception is not a feeling either of pleasure or pain, nor a desire. And pleasure and pain, and desires, they clearly see, are not perceptions. Hence classing them together would be improper, and create confusion. It would be confounding things which differ, and destroying all those distinctions which are necessary to the acquirement of scientific knowledge. For a person has no more than a confused notion of things, who does not make distinctions, where there are differences; or point out the difference between one thing and another. As perceptions and affections generically differ, philosophers have distinguished them, and formed them into distinct classes; and so they have admitted the existence of *two* faculties. *And for the same reason they admit two, they ought to grant there are three faculties.* For when we attend to the affections and to volitions, it is evident there is a generic difference between them. It is evident that pain, pleasure, and desires, are not volitions; and have no similarity to those voluntary exertions, which produce effects on the body, and in other things around us. For those affections do not immediately produce any external effects; they are effects themselves, produced by the heart, and are either virtuous or vicious. For it has been shown that vice and virtue belong to the heart only, and its operations, or affections. There is, therefore, no more propriety in classing the affections and volitions together, than in making but one class of affections and perceptions. The affections and volitions so widely differ, that they naturally divide themselves into two distinct, general classes." (pp. 92-93.)

These three divisions, which correspond to the Kantian distribution of mental operations into Thinking, Feeling, and Willing, Burton calls *Understanding, Taste,* and *Will.*

The *Understanding* "is undefinable; for two reasons. (1) It is an individual property. (2) It is simple in its nature. And of individual, simple existences, no one can give a logical definition. . . *Perceptions* are the operations of this faculty. (pp. 20, 21.) Simple apprehension as an act of the mind, or the perception of an object, Conception. . . Memory, reason, judgment, and conscience . . . are operations of this faculty. This is true with respect to imagination. . . Apprehension, conception, judgment, reason, memory, conscience, imagination, fancy, which are words abundantly used by philosophers who treat upon the intellectual powers of the mind, are names by which the acts or operations of the understanding are designated. For the understanding is the only intellectual faculty belonging to the mind. And when we attend to the meaning of these words, as applied to acts of the mind, it is obvious they cannot designate any other operations, than those which I call

perceptions. . . Being similar, of the same kind, they constitute one general class of operations. (pp. 50-51.)

"*Taste* is another faculty of the mind, distinct from the understanding and the will . . . like the understanding, undefinable, being a simple property. . . Taste is that faculty by
which the mind is pleased or disgusted by the objects which affect it. . . If we had not the bodily sense, which is called taste,
food would neither please or disgust us. By a mental taste, the
mind is pleased or displeased with all objects with which it is
conversant. There is a great similarity between that bodily
sense, called taste, and this mental faculty, by means of which
all objects affect us in an agreeable or disagreeable manner. On
account of this similarity, this mental faculty is called the taste.
I know of no other word, which will, according to its common
acceptation, more fully express the nature of this faculty. And
for this reason I use it. The word of God calls this faculty, the
heart. . . Do we infer, from our perception, the faculty which
is called the understanding? Then from our feelings, we as
safely infer the faculty we call taste, or the heart. . . [It] is
a feeling faculty. . . Feeling is the spring of action. . . As it
is evident, if we were as incapable of pleasure and pain as stones
are, that we should be inactive beings it follows that feelings
give rise to all the actions of moral agents. . . Taste is a moral
faculty. Here is the fountain of all vice and virtue. . . The
understanding is a perceiving faculty, but is never the subject of
sensations. It never feels anything. The faculty of taste is a
feeling faculty. It never perceives anything. . . These are evident and essential differences between the understanding and
the taste; and show us that they are totally distinct faculties,
from which operations of a different nature proceed. (pp.
53-61.)

"Rhetoricians commonly define Taste, to be a power of deriving pleasure or pain from objects of nature and art; and
consider beauty and sublimity to be the sources of the greatest

pleasures afforded to it. I believe they have never considered this power, as they call it, a distinct faculty of the mind; nor attended to its operations in this light. . . To me it appears very clear, that their taste, and what is called by the same name in these essays, are the same power, property or faculty. They have reflected great light on this branch of intellectual philosophy. But they have treated the subject . . . in a too restricted and limited sense. (pp. 249-250.)

"The faculty of taste is the most important property of the mind. It is the seat of all our pleasures and pains; contains all the principles of action, which govern man; it is the fountain of vice and virtue; and according to its nature such is the moral character of men and of all intelligent beings; and according to its nature when we bid farewell to life, such will be our endless state beyond the grave. (pp. 253-254.)

"Scarcely any writer, that I now recollect, has considered the heart and *will* to be distinct faculties. They have generally been treated as one and the same. Yet I hope to make it appear that they are distinct faculties, and ought not to be blended with the understanding. . . There is no adaptedness in matter for the operations of thinking and feeling. And if the mind were not prepared to be the subject of those operations termed perceptions, feelings, and volitions, it could no more perceive, feel, and choose, than matter itself can. But the mind does think, feel, and choose. These are facts, which prove undeniably, that it is prepared for these operations. And a particular preparedness, fitness, or adaptedness for that kind of operations called volitions, is what I mean and understand by the term *will*, considered as a faculty of the mind. Some will say, this is no definition. I grant it is not. It is impossible to define simple ideas." (pp. 84-85.)

Memory, judgment, reason, and conscience are shown to be specific forms of perception.

"It will be granted, that *remembering* is an operation of the mind. . . The more this subject may be examined, the more obvious it will appear, that remembering, considered as an operation of the mind, is a perception of an object. And this perception differs no more from any other perception, than any two perceptions differ from each other. . . Though all the operations of the mind are perceptions of objects, and being alike ought to be classed together, they are subdivided into several distinct species of operations. . . On account of these differences between the objects remembered and those which are not, all these perceptions of past objects are formed into a distinct class, and to this class or division the name memory is given. (pp. 27-29.)

"*Judgment* is agreed to be an act of the mind. It is that act by which one thing is affirmed or denied of another; or it is an assent to the truth of a proposition. And this assent . . . is an act of the mind. But what act or operation of the mind is it? Is it a sensation, or a volition? This is never pretended. It must be a perception. For we experience no other operations than perceptions, sensations, and volitions. All our operations may be included in one or the other of these general classes. (pp. 30-31.)

"*Reason* . . . is a power of the understanding to infer one proposition from another. . . In this process of the mind none of its operations are employed but perceptions. . . As the objects of perception differ is particular respects, they are divided into several classes, to designate and remind us of this difference. . . Hence the reason, why different names are given to the same operations of the understanding, is not because they differ in their kind or nature, but because the objects of those operations differ from each other. (pp. 31-34.)

"The operations of *conscience* are perceptions, and do not differ in their nature from other perceptions, which are operations of the understanding. But the objects perceived, are different. . . Those perceptions of the understanding, which have the right or wrong of our hearts and conduct, or in a word our duty, for their object, are classed together and called *conscience*. Or conscience may be thus defined: it is the understanding itself, when it takes cognizance of our motives and actions, compares them with the standard of duty, and then acquits or condemns. (pp. 43, 49.)

"All the operations of the understanding form one general class called perceptions. This general class of operations is divided into several specific classes. And each specific class has some name given it, by which it is known; as simple perception, memory, judgment, reason and conscience. And the difference among the *objects* of perception, is the reason why our perceptions are formed into distinct classes." (p. 52.)

The operations of Taste are the Affections and the Passions.

"The affections and passions comprise all the operations of this faculty. The affections and passions do not differ in their nature. The real difference is circumstantial. When any emotion is suddenly excited, and is strong and vivid, and is soon moderated, it is called a passion. And those sensations, which gradually increase, which continue and abide, are termed affections. (p. 71.)

"Each affection and passion contains two operations; a sensation, either pleasant or painful; and a desire to obtain the object, if agreeable, or to avoid it, if disagreeable. These two operations, sensation and desire, combine to form every affection and passion. (p. 83.)

"Our primary affections form one class of the operations of our taste; secondary affections, a second; and our malignant passions, a third. These three classes include all the operations of this faculty. It is presumed no one can name any affection or passion, which is not clearly contained in one or another of the classes I have named." (p. 81.)

The appetites are enumerated, and are shown to be species of the genus taste.

"1. An appetite for food. . . This appetite is attended with three distinct operations; uneasiness, desire and pleasure. . .

"2. The natural affections . . . include the parental, filial, and fraternal affections. The propensity to exercise them may be called a particular and distinct appetite. . .

"3. The propensity of the different sexes for social intercourse. . .

"4. Pity. The object of this appetite is the distress and misery of mankind. Experience teaches, that it is a very active principle, and a law of our nature, like other appetites. . .

"5. An appetite to be pleased with novelty. . .

"6. Another appetite with which Adam was created is termed benevolent. The character of God, the happiness of intelligent beings, divine truths and doctrines, holiness, the law and service of God, are the class of objects with which this appetite is pleased. This is lost by our apostacy from God. Hence the reason why men in a natural state are not pleased with this class of objects. . . Whether these are all the appetites implanted in us by our Maker, or not, I will not affirm. These appear to me to be the principal, if not the whole. There are some appetites which are acquired, commonly called habits; as the love of labour, intemperance, and the like. . . All the appetites, which we have enumerated, may by use and cultivation, be increased; they may also in certain ways be diminished." (pp. 63-66.)

"We are to remember the heart is a feeling faculty, the subject of pleasant and painful sensations. And if the appetites were not so different and distinct, the loss of one would annihilate all feeling in us. . . Now, if the several species were not so different and distinct, that destroying one species would not be destroying another; the annihilation of one species would annihilate every other, or destroy the genus. . . And the appetites, conjointly viewed, constitute the faculty termed taste or the heart. (p. 68.)

"Some may find it difficult to perceive a difference between an appetite, and the faculty called taste. The real difference is the same, as between a species and a genus. A genus includes all the species under it. The faculty of taste is a genus, which includes all the appetites. Hence an appetite differs from the taste, as a species does from its genus. . . The taste is a fitness to feel pleasure or pain in view of all objects; and a single appetite is suited to be affected with only one class of objects." (pp. 401-2.)

Finally, a careful distinction is made between the will and the feelings.

"I shall now proceed to show the difference between the operations of the *heart*, and those of the *will*. Here let is be remembered, that pleasant and painful sensations, and the desires which accompany them, are the operations of the heart. And volitions are the exertions of the will, to produce the effects necessary to gratify the feelings of the heart. . .

"1. Neither a pleasant or painful sensation is a volition.

"2. Volitions and desires are not operations of the same faculty. . . We may desire what we do not will. . . Hence *a desire is not a volition. . . And every person's experience daily decides this dispute.*

"3. Whether objects shall please or disgust us, does not depend on any thing in us, except our nature; but whether they shall be chosen or not, depends on our pleasure.

"4. Observe, that vice and virtue have their seat in the heart, not in the will. This constitutes an essential difference between these two faculties. . . The heart or taste with its affections are the primary principle of action. . . The will is only an executive faculty." (pp. 87-91.)

This was the unique contribution of Burton to the growing science of psychology, and while he agreed with Edwards' conclusions, he provided the psychological refutation of his main argument.

"Proceeding on the supposition that we have only the two faculties named, it is impossible for us to be governed by motives." (p. 404.)

His summary expresses his position most succinctly:

"The numerous operations of the understanding I have called by one general name, perceptions. I think I have made it evident, that every operation of this faculty is a *perception*. Those perceptions are divided into distinct, specific classes, termed reason, memory, conscience, judgment, imagination. And the numerous operations of the taste or heart, are known by the name of affections. This general class is divided into several specific classes, termed primary, secondary, and malignant affections. And the numerous operations of the will are known by the term *volitions*. This class does not admit of any divisions. These three general classes, *perceptions, affections, and volitions,* include all the operations of the mind. It is presumed no person can name an operation, which is not included in one or the other of these classes. As these several classes generically differ, for the same reasons that two faculties have been admitted to belong to the human mind, it is necessary to admit a third." (pp. 93-94.)

The period from 1776 to 1827 thus included original work on the part of such Americans as Rush and Burton, as well as the anachronistic note of scholasticism sounded by Gros, and the desperate vindication of Locke attempted by Beasley. But the most persistent influence was the importation of the Scottish philosophy by Witherspoon, and the example set by Stanhope Smith of an adequate development of psychological doctrine in an extended treatise. The texts of Reid, Stewart, Beattie and, later, of Brown, flowed into the country in a continuous stream, but there was already a marked feeling that these were not systematic expositions of mental philosophy. Such a comment was made by Ezra Stiles Ely (1786-1861) in a thoughtful little book entitled "Conversations on the Science of the Human Mind":

"A systematic treatise . . . is greatly to be desired. Such an one does not exist; for Dr. Reid, who has excelled all other writers on this subject, employed himself rather in demolishing an old fabrick, than in building up a new one. Professor Stewart is but an elegant commentator upon Reid, without originality, and without any comprehensive arrangement of the topics of mental science." [64]

Such a treatise appeared in 1827 from the pen of Thomas C. Upham. It was the first of a series of comprehensive, well-organized works by Americans, and antedated any similar texts in Great Britain by a quarter to half a century.[65] The Era of American Textbooks was about to open.

The Era of American Textbooks, 1827-1861

In 1847 Robert Vaughan, the scholarly editor of the *British Quarterly Review*, wrote these words:

"Within the last ten or twenty years . . . bold, original, and profound thinkers have arisen on the other side of the Atlantic, and have published the results of their thinking to the world. They have observed, and theorized on the momentous problems presented in the phenomena of human nature and its relations; they have analyzed and generalized these phenomena, and have contributed the fruit of such efforts to the general stock of knowledge on these interesting and important subjects." [66]

The thirty-four years between the appearance of the "first original and comprehensive contribution of American scholarship to modern psychology," [67] and the violent set-back of the Civil War, are marked by the gradually maturing system of *Thomas C. Upham*,[68] the "Sully" of America, the work of *Frederick Rauch* and *S. S. Schmucker*,[69] German-Americans both, the philosophical system of *Asa Mahan* of Oberlin, based on Coleridge, Cousin and Kant, "three luminaries of the first order in the sphere of philosophy," [70] and the super-Kantian transcendentalism of *Laurens P. Hickok*,[71] in which "we pass from the facts of experience wholly out of it, and seek for the rational of experience itself in the necessary and universal principles which must be conditional for all facts of a possible experience." [72] After this breath-taking rational psychology raised to the *n*th degree, we find the period closing calmly with the genial "Intellectual Philosophy" of President *Francis Wayland* of Brown, and with a monument of scholarship in the form of a superb manual of "Mental Philosophy" by *Joseph Haven* of Amherst. These works together with many others of minor importance, which will receive passing mention at appropriate points, represent the "non-existent" American psychology of a single period before 1890. How worthily they represent it will appear in the sequel.

a. *Thomas C. Upham*,[73] *1799-1872*

It is a practical lesson in methodology to compare the first three forms of Upham's Elements, and watch him shape his material into the beautifully symmetrical system which he finally evolved. It is interesting too to see the progress of his thought with respect to the distribution of the mental operations. In his first book, "Elements of Intellectual Philosophy," [74] he refuses to accept any definite classification, fearing that he might yield to the temptation to force his data into ready-made categories.

"It has been thought best in this work to avoid adopting any general division, which has at least this favorable circumstance attending it, that we thereby avoid becoming pledged and holden in support of any particular writer or system. The great object we have before us is to ascertain facts in regard to the mind; the arrangement of those facts, and any speculations, which are not directly founded upon them, are subordinate points of consideration. And there is the greater reason for pursuing this course, when it is remembered that men have ever discovered a strong tendency to make premature generalizations. It flatters their pride; and in thus doing they are urged forward by the influence of a puerile vanity more than by the pure love of truth." (2nd Ed., p. 50.)

In his two-volume work entitled "Elements of Mental Philosophy," [75] (he had already discarded the term "intellectual" as too narrow),[76] he presents the most cogent arguments for the distribution of the operations of the mind into *two* great classes, citing the authority of writers on mental science, the testimony of language, and the evidence of consciousness.[77] He concludes with a brief résumé of classifications, and finds himself authorized to consider "the states, exercises, or acts of the mind . . . under the *two* general heads of *Intellectual* and *Sentient.*" [78]

In May, 1834, Upham wrote the "Preface to his Philosophical and Practical Treatise on the Will" (forming the third volume of his System of Mental Philosophy).[79] In working over the data of the mental life, he had found that a twofold division of the faculties was inadequate, and he had also in the meantime come upon Burton's "Essays." The result was a *tri-partite division*, which from then on completely dominated his system and dictated its internal arrangements. In his own words,

"Although we properly ascribe to the human soul the attributes of oneness or indivisibility, there is abundant reason for saying, that its nature can never be fully understood by contemplating it solely under one aspect. There are, accordingly, *three* prominent and well-defined points of view, in which the mind may be contemplated, viz., the Intellect, the Sensibilities, and the Will; otherwise expressed by the phrases INTELLECTUAL, SENTIENT, and VOLUNTARY states of the mind. Whatever truly and appropriately belongs to the intellect, has something peculiar and characteristic of it, which shuts it off from the domain of the sensibilities; and whatever has the nature of a volition has a position apart both from the intellectual and the sentient. This is a fundamental arrangement, which, when properly and fully carried out and applied, includes the whole soul. To the one or the other of these general heads, every thing involved in our mental existence, may be referred. In fully exhausting, therefore, these topics, we may justly count upon having completed the exploration of the mental constitution. When we have done this, nothing remains to be said. The work is finished. The depths of the mind have been entered; the heights have been ascended; the boundaries have been set up." [80]

The influence of Burton would be manifest, even without the extended citation which Upham makes from the "Essays." [81] Now that his mind is finally made up, he finds the most conclusive arguments for the threefold division,[82]

"premising, at the same time, that the whole of this work, while it is based in a good degree on this fundamental division, will be found to furnish incidental evidence throughout of its truth." (p. 52.)

Vaughan comments thus:

"The principles of scientific classification are now better understood than formerly. . . The arrangement of mental phenomena, or the division of the mind into faculties, etc., and the application to these of a terminology based on strictly scientific principles, form, it must be admitted, difficult undertakings. . . Professor Upham seems to be fully aware of the difficulties attendant on this matter. In several admirable passages, directly on the point, he fully admits the imperfections and inconsistencies which characterize our classifications of mental states or phenomena.[83] Notwithstanding these modest statements, the Professor's general division of the states of mind into intellectual, sentient, and voluntary, appears to us one of the best—the least objectionable that has yet been advanced. The classification is a natural, a distinct, and an exhaustive one; and the nomenclature happily selected, and of extensive application in the details of the Science. The terms, as names of kinds, express, with considerable accuracy, real distinctions in mental states—distinctions which consciousness authorizes. . . Many points in the subdivisions or minor classifications of Upham are also, in our opinion, calculated, as well by their scientific accuracy as their practical application, to facilitate the study of mental philosophy." [84]

Equally interesting and instructive is his use of sources, and arrangement of the material he took lavishly from his predecessors.

"Professor Upham's system is based upon the Anglo-Scottish philosophy, though it contains many important modifications, both original, and adopted from continental psychology. . . . The larger portion of these alterations, . . . we are disposed to regard as improvements, and think they will constitute instructive and valuable contributions to our existing mental science." [85]

His first work is based on Locke,[86] influenced however from the first by the "primary truths" of Reid and Stewart.[87] In 1831 he discarded Locke as his major source, finding himself more influenced by the Scottish school and by the French writers, with whom he was unusually familiar.[88] He was curiously untouched by Cousin,[89] mentions Kant only once, although he was a good German scholar,[90] and completed his system before the writings of Hamilton reached America. He had no precedent for the arrangement of his topics, and his greatest merit lies in the way in which he shaped up his material,[91] laid it out in an orderly succession,[92] and presented it so attractively that his books went through numerous editions,[93] were used widely in academies and colleges,[94] and were still printed and offered for sale in 1886.

Upham was an eclectic, borrowing freely from the ancient writers, from British, French, German, and American authors both in the field of mental science and in general literature.

"It has been my object, aided by the views and researches which have characterized the labours of various philosophical sects, to give a condensed, but just and impartial, account of most of the leading principles of Mental Philosophy, so far as they appear to be ascertained and recognized at the present time. The Work, accordingly, is essentially Eclectic in its character; and, as such, can neither incur the discredit, nor claim the honour, of belonging exclusively to any of the great Philosophical Schools, although it does not hesitate to acknowledge its indebtedness to all." (p. iii.)

He was greatly interested in science, and especially in travel, showing a particular fondness for finding illustrations in the reports of Captain Cook, Mungo Park, and other world travelers. He quotes from at least ten periodicals and reports of institutions and learned societies, as well as from the standard encyclopaedias of the time. He closes each section of his magnum opus with a thoughtful discussion of pathological conditions,[95] and in 1840 he published the first systematic text in America on abnormal psychology.[96]

Professor Upham announces his intention of writing a systematic but elementary text for the beginner in mental science.

"It has been my desire and endeavor . . . to give a concise, but correct view of the prominent principles in Intellectual Philosophy, so far as they seemed at present to be settled. The statement of these principles is attended with a conspicuous summary of the facts and arguments, on which they are based, together with occasional remarks on the objections, which have been made from time to time. In selecting facts in confirmation of the principles laid down, I have sought those, which not only had relation to the point in hand, but which promised a degree of *interest for young minds*. Simplicity and uniformity of style have been aimed at, although in a few instances the statement of the writers referred to have been admitted with only slight variations, when it was thought they had been peculiarly happy in them." [97]

His method is to be Baconian induction. As admirably stated by the editor of the *British Quarterly Review:*

"With [Upham and Schmucker] philosophy is concerned only with the phenomenal and the relative (i.e., not with problems 'beyond the province of philosophical investigation'). Whatever we may think of some of their doctrines, the general anxiety to restrict their researches to proper subjects must commend their works to our attention.

"What is the method pursued? . . . Philosophers now seem to be agreed, theoretically at least, that the only safe method of inquiry is the inductive process. . . Both Upham and Schmucker professedly adopt the inductive method. They distinctly avow this. But have they adhered to these professions? Without asserting that they have, with rigid uniformity, in the discussion of every question, we bear willing testimony to the general faithfulness their inquiries evince to the requirements of the laws of inductive reasoning. Both have made the revelation of consciousness the field of investigation, they have acknowledged it as the ultimate and legitimate authority, by appealing to it at every step of their inquiries—have confided in its reports, and endeavoured to arrive at authorized generalizations of the facts given in it. *The work of Upham forms, perhaps, the most consistent specimen of the application of this mode of investigation to mental science in our language.* Free from the trammels of sects and system, imbued with a disposition to seize upon what he conceives to be true, wherever he may find it, and directed by such a portion of theoretical design as serves to give pertinency and scientific accuracy to his inquiries and reasonings, he has produced a book that displays great labour in the collection of facts, patient and comprehensive habits of thought in their generalization, and clear scientific arrangement in the combination of the whole into systematic form." [98]

He begins his work with a discussion of primary truths, the immateriality of the mind, the laws of belief, and a general classification of mental operations. His system may be shown schematically as follows:

I. *Intellect*
    1. Intellectual States of External Origin
    2. Intellectual States of Internal Origin
    3. Pathology of the Intellect

II. *The Sensibilities*
    1. Natural or Pathematic
        (1) Emotions
        (2) Desires
    2. Moral
        (1) Emotions of Approval and Disapproval
        (2) Feelings of Moral Obligation
        (3) Pathology of the Affections

III. *The Will*

His treatment of the intellectual states of external origin covers the general heads of Sensation and Perception,[99] Conception, Abstraction, and Attention. In connection with the first two of these topics he has most suggestive chapters on Habits of Sensation and Perception and Muscular Habits. He finds Attention a convenient point to lead off into a consideration of Dreaming and Somnambulism.

The intellectual states of internal origin comprise Original and Relative Suggestion (Thomas Brown's terminology for Intuition and Judgment),[100] Consciousness, Memory, Reasoning, and Imagination. In this connection the Association of Ideas is discussed, and both the primary laws as originally formulated by Aristotle, and the secondary laws laid down by Thomas Brown are fully treated. The discussion of Casual Association is particularly ingenious.

"Another important question in modern philosophy—association of ideas, is admirably discussed by Upham. . . It is well known that, in some of our recent systems of philosophy, the principle of association has been extensively applied as a means of explaining mental phenomena. Indeed, we think it has been pushed beyond its legitimate province. That acute and original thinker, James Mill, in our opinion, attempted to explain phenomena by this principle, for an explication of which it is wholly incompetent. Upham restricts the application of association to narrower limits. *His observations contain a more full, scientific, and consistent explanation of the subject, than that of his predecessors in the school with which he stands most closely connected.*" [101]

This is Upham's summary of the first great division of his work.

"Such is the view of the Intellect, in its normal action (not of the mind as a whole, but of the perceptive or intellective part of the mind), which seems to us accordant with the facts of personal consciousness, and with the record of the mind, as it discloses itself in the observation of others around us, and in human history. Not of the Will, and not of the Sensibilities, which remain to be considered, but of the Intellect alone, developing itself into the two great forms of the Sensuous and the Super-sensuous, otherwise known as Sensationalism and Intellectualism; and not only in the successive cognitive powers—all related to each other, and yet all comparatively independent—of Sensation, Perception, Conceptivity, Abstraction, Intuition, Consciousness, Relative Suggestion, and Reasoning, but also, closely related to, and yet discriminate from, the sources of cognition, in the great power of Imagination; together with the Auxiliary powers, which so greatly diversify and enhance the mental action, of Habit, Attention, Association, and Memory.

If our inquiries stopped here, and we had nothing further to say, we could not fail to be impressed with the dignity and greatness of man's nature, and with the wisdom and goodness of the Being from whence he came." (pp. 449-450.)

The second volume of the definitive edition is devoted to the Sensibilities and the Will.

"In this part of his labours, taken as a whole, there is less exact agreement with previous writers, and more originality— greater modification of extant doctrine. . . In proceeding to treat of the desires, he points out more clearly than previous writers their relative place in the order of mental states, as subsequent to intellections and emotions. . . Another marked peculiarity in this part of Upham's investigations is his exposition of the instinctive and voluntary operation of these feelings. He shows that all these, except the instincts, are susceptible of existing in states that possess a moral character, as well as in passive or pathological states. . . [It is here] that we think our author has rendered the greatest service to mental science, by the original and masterly exposition he has given of man's moral nature. The connection, the mutual dependence of those two great problems in mental and moral philosophy—what are man's moral susceptibilities—his moral nature? and that other, the determination of which constitutes ethics, properly so-called —what is right action? are admirably explained and illustrated." [102]

The relation of the Sensibilities to the Intellect, and the progressive movement of the Sensibilities themselves are most ingeniously laid out.

"The *Intellect* or Understanding comes first in order, and furnishes the basis of action to the other departments of the

mind. . . As a general thing, there is, and can be no movement of the sensibilities, no such thing as an emotion, desire, or
feeling of moral obligation, without an antecedent action of
the intellect. (II, pp. 23, 25-6.)

"The *Sensibilities* . . . will clearly be found to separate
themselves into the great divisions of the *Natural* or Pathematic,[103] and the *Moral*. . . The exercise of the natural or
pathematic sensibilities is the first in order of time. . . [This
division] considers objects chiefly as they have a relation to ourselves; the other [moral] as they relate to all possible existences. . . The one asks what is good, the other what is right.
. . We shall find this portion of our sentient nature resolving
itself into the subordinate divisions of the *Emotions* and *Desires*. These two classes of mental states follow each other in
the order in which they have been named; the Emotions first,
which are exceedingly numerous and various; and then the
Desires, embracing under the latter term, the *Appetites, Propensities*, and *Affections*. . . As we cannot be pleased or displeased without some antecedent perception of knowledge of
the thing which we are pleased or displeased with, so we cannot desire to possess or avoid anything without having laid the
foundation of such desire in the existence of some antecedent
emotion. . . The moral sensibilities divide themselves in a
manner entirely analogous. . . The first class of mental states
which presents itself to our notice under this general head is
that of *Moral Emotions* . . . followed by another class of
moral feelings, which may be designated as *Obligatory Feelings*, or feelings of moral obligation. . . (pp. 29, 31, 32, 35,
36.)

"Emotions always occupy a place between intellections or
acts of the intellect and the desires, if they are natural emotions; and between intellections and feelings of moral obligation, if they are moral emotions." (pp. 40-41.)

The scheme may be tabulated as follows:

THE SENSIBILITIES

I. Natural (or Pathematic)
  1. Emotions
    (1) Beauty
    (2) Sublimity
    (3) Ludicrous
    (4) Others (Cheerfulness, sorrow, surprise, dissatisfaction, modesty, regard, reverence, etc.)
  2. Desires
    (1) Instincts (Respiration, swallowing, instinctive acts of self-preservation, of resentment, etc.)
    (2) Appetites (Hunger, thirst, etc.)
    (3) Propensities (Self-preservation, curiosity, imitation, desire for power, veracity, self-love, sociality)
    (4) Affections
      a. Malevolent (Anger, peevishness, envy, jealousy, revenge, fear)
      b. Benevolent (Love, humanity, patriotism, pity, sympathy, gratitude, love of God)
II. Moral
  1. Emotions
    (1) Approval and Disapproval
    (2) Feelings of moral beauty and sublimity
  2. Feelings of Obligation
III. Pathology of the Sensibilities

A cognition is followed in certain cases by an emotion, either natural or moral. A natural emotion is followed by a desire, a moral emotion by a feeling of obligation. Either tends to issue in action. Desires are further analyzed into Instincts, Appetites, Propensities, and Affections. At any one of these levels, habits of the Sensibilities may be formed, resulting in organized systems of sentiments and character traits. Moral education is education of the Sensibilities. Imperfect or disordered action of the Sensibilities is systematically treated.

It is extremely difficult to give a definition of the Emotions in words. They are simple mental states analogous to a simple sensation such as blue, which is indefinable to one who has not had it or who is blind.

"The fact of their entire simplicity necessarily renders them undefinable. . . We do not suppose indeed that any one is ignorant of what is meant when we have occasion to speak of an emotion, whether it be an emotion of melancholy, of cheerfulness, of surprise, of grandeur, or of some other kind. . . We are dependent for a knowledge of the interior and essential nature of emotions, not upon verbal explanations and definitions, which are inadequate to the communication of such knowledge, but upon consciousness." (II, pp. 39-40.)

They arise spontaneously in the presence of the appropriate stimulus. They are prompt and rapid in their origin, are evanescent and extremely varied. "We must take it for granted that the mind has an original susceptibility of such emotions." The appropriate stimulus is defined in the case of each of the emotions described, and the subsequent behavior of the emotion is shown to be modified by association. The importance of the susceptibilities in human life is eloquently described.

"If man had been formed of intellect alone, of cold and unimpassioned perceptivity; if he could merely have perceived, compared, associated, and reasoned, without a solitary emotion or desire, without sorrow for suffering or sympathy in joy; in a

word, if he had been all head and no heart, the human soul
would have shown not only a different, but a depressed and inferior aspect, compared with what it does at present. . . It is
in this department of the mind we find the causes which render
men restless and inquisitive, which prompt to efforts both good
and evil, and make the wide world a theatre, where vice and
virtue, hope and fear, and joy and suffering, mingle in perpetual conflict.

"A knowledge of human nature, in the common apprehension of the phrase, does not so much imply a knowledge of the
powers of perception and reasoning as a knowledge of the
springs of action, back of the intellect, which, in the shape of
the emotions and passions, give an impulse and a character to
the conduct both of individuals and communities." (II, pp.
26-27.)

The last great division of the mind is called the *Will*.

"The mind, both in its internal constitution and in its adap-
tation to outward objects, is evidently framed for movement.
It was never meant to be essentially dormant, either in a state
of unconsciousness or of mere contemplation and emotion. . .
The immediate and proximate seat and source of action is the
Will. (II, pp. 462.)

"The intellect . . . is, in no case, in direct contact with the
Will. When, therefore, we speak of the operation of the intellect upon the Will, we mean an indirect or circuitous operation; that is to say, one which is carried on through the medium
of the sensibilities. . . We find the intellections in contact, or,
more properly speaking, in immediate proximity, with the emotions. . . The natural progress of the mind, in bringing the
Will into action, is from intellections to emotions . . . and
then from emotions to desires. . . It is in Desires . . . that
we find a class of immediate antecedents to the acts of the Will.
. . Volition is the great result, to which [all departments of

the mind] contribute, and with which they all, therefore, sustain an established connection, though not with the same degree of nearness." (pp. 465-6, 469, 474, 476, 477, 478.)

"Here let us interpose a word of caution. It is not to be inferred, when we speak of one part of the mind in distinction from another, and of passing from one part or power to another, that the mind is a congeries of distinct existences, or that it is, in any literal sense of the terms, susceptible of division. Varieties of action do not necessarily imply a want of unity in the principle from which they originate. *The mental principle,* therefore, *is indivisible.* In itself it is truly and essentially a unity, *though multiplied,* in a manner calculated to excite the greatest astonishment, *in its modes of application. It is merely one of these modes of its application,* or, rather, one of these modes of its exercise, *which is indicated by the term Will.* Accordingly, the term Will is not meant to express anything separate from the mind, but nevertheless embodies and expresses the great fact, founded upon psychical existence developing itself through fixed psychical relations, of the mind's ability to operate in a new and specific way." (p. 485.)

Desires and volitions are most carefully distinguished. The Will is discussed at length under the headings of Laws of the Will, Freedom of the Will, and Power of the Will, the last head giving an opportunity for an appropriate digression into a treatment of the fully integrated personality. The whole section is admirably summarized by Foster: [104]

"The laws considered are those of causality, those found in the moral government, those implied in the prescience of the Deity and the foresight of men, in the sciences relating to human conduct, and those intimated by consciousness, and the influence of motives. . . He means by freedom a true power of causality. . . While he defers the whole matter of the consistency of the will's subjection to law with the fact of freedom, he affirms that they are consistent, using Emmons' appeal to reason for the idea of law, and to consciousness for the knowledge of freedom."

A spirit of seriousness, piety, and fair-mindedness pervades the whole work. The author stresses the genetic approach,[105] makes much of child psychology,[106] and shows a deep interest in anthropology.[107] His remarks on education may be read with interest and profit today, and his position on moral education is most timely.

"While no one presumes to assert that moral education is unimportant, it must be ackuowledged that it has been exceedingly neglected."

This sentence and the rest of the passage (II, p. 389) might have been written in the present decade of the twentieth century. The following statement has a modern, even Thorndikean touch:

"Our moral principles, however correct they may be, will be but of little value to us, unless they are put to practice by being incorporated into the daily and hourly series of living acts." (II, p. 399.)

He devotes sixty pages of the first volume to an admirable discussion of language, and takes up educational applications in connection with the discussion of each mental operation. Like most of the "early psychologists" he anticipates many ideas commonly supposed to be modern, for example:

Mental Set. "In all arguments, whether moral or demonstrative, there is some general subject on which the evidence is made to bear; there is some point in particular to be examined.

In reference to these general outlines, we have a prevailing and permanent desire. This desire is not only a great help in giving quickness and strength to the laws of association, but exercises also a very considerable indirect influence in giving an appropriate character to the thoughts which are suggested by those laws." (I, p. 381.)

Individual Differences. "Making allowance for those constitutional differences which pervade every part of the mental structure." (II, p. 26.)

Introversion and Extraversion. "The law holds good . . . in respect to original differences of emotion and passion, or, as it is more commonly expressed, of disposition. It will help to make us understood if we allude briefly, in this part of the subject, to two different classes of persons. One of the descriptions of men which we have in view is composed of those . . . who are constitutionally of a pensive and melancholy turn. From their earliest life they have shown a fondness for seclusion. . . The other class are naturally of a lively and cheerful temperament. If they delight in nature, it is not in solitude, but in the company of others." (I, pp. 321-322.)

Rationalization. "When vices are committed by near friends, by a brother or a parent . . . our prepossessions in favour of the persons who have committed the crime suggest a thousand circumstances, which seem to us to alleviate its aggravation. We frame for them a multitude of plausible excuses." (II, pp. 351-352.)

Emergence of suppressed desires in perverted forms. "By a thousand circumstances and in thousands of instances, the feelings are wrenched from their natural position, and shoot forth and show themselves in misplaced and disproportionate forms. Casual associations, in the shape of antipathies, fears, aversions, prepositions, remorse, etc., are found seated in many a mind, which is otherwise unembarrassed and unexceptionable in its action. . . If it were otherwise, how could a man that would willingly face a thousand men in battle, tremble at a mouse, a squirrel, a thunder-shower, at the trivial circumstance of placing the left slipper on the right foot, or any other very trifling thing. And yet such instances are without number." (II, p. 446.)

James-Lange Theory of Emotions. "These passions, like all the other natural and implanted passions, reveal themselves outwardly by certain natural signs, such as a kindling eye, a flushed countenance, violent gesticulation, and a hurried and raised tone of voice. And it is an interesting fact that the suppression of the outward signs which, in general, is a thing entirely within our power, operates powerfully to suppress the internal passion." (II, p. 398.)

Upham's style is lucid and generally sober, although at times he lets himself go in a burst of pulpit eloquence. As Flugel says of Sully,[108] he had a gift for clear and ordered exposition, and his books filled a great need, and stimulated an interest in a subject which Ely had said in 1819 was so full of metaphysical jargon and nonsense, that people believed "that one who would become a metaphysician must renounce common sense." [109]

In short, he wrote a good textbook, and, as Boring says, "A writer of textbooks is not without his place in the history of science, since he gives knowledge explicit form and diffuses it." Let the candid editor of the *British Quarterly Review* sum up.

"The lucid arrangement of the subjects in Upham's work, the candour everywhere displayed, the true spirit of inductive investigation which characterizes all his inquiries, and the simple, easy, and natural, yet vigorous and precise style in which his work is written, render it eminently suitable for the purposes of instruction. It is, in other respects, admirably suited for an elementary work; and we think its circulation in this country would contribute to revive and invigorate a taste for the cultivation of sound philosophy. We earnestly recommend it to the attention of the student of mental philosophy." [110]

b. *Frederick Rauch (1806-1841) and S. S. Schmucker (1799-1873)*

Before the appearance of the next important American text in psychology, several minor works which deserve passing notice were brought to public attention. A little book called "The Mental Guide" [111] popularized a reduced version of Locke as an introduction to practical exercises in literary composition. It designs

"to make a proper division of Metaphysical Principles as advanced by Locke, Stewart, and others, and apply them in some measure to use—that the science may be entered upon with less difficulty than before." (p. iv.)

Francis Wayland brought out his "Moral Philosophy" [112] in 1835. In 1847 it was in its thirty-first thousand, and by 1860, 130,000 copies had been sold. The *Fowler Brothers*, proclaiming that "to Americanize whatever in science and the arts, is capable of improving or adorning the mind, or of otherwise benefiting mankind, is no less the duty, than it would prove the glory, of every American citizen," and lamenting the spirit of literary servility that had confined everything *phrenological* to a "reprint or a substantial copy of some foreign work," proceeded to do their scientific and artistic duty and add to their glory by issuing the first of a long series of works on phrenology [113] that caught the public fancy and held it for many decades.

Mrs. *Elizabeth Ricord*,[114] Principal of the Geneva Female Seminary, "with the strongest sentiments of affection for the Youth of her country, more especially those of her own sex," presented "to those, whose future influence will soon be identified with all the objects most hallowed by us, our literary, political, moral, and religious Institutions," a volume on the "Elements of the Philosophy of Mind, applied to the Development of Thought and Feeling." [115] The style is florid and rhetorical, but the book contains many practical illustrations of psychological points. It is a true product of the "Sentimental Years," bordering on the "Fabulous Forties."

In the same year, 1839, *Leicester A. Sawyer*,[116] A.M., published a "Critical Exposition of Mental Philosophy, or the First Principles of Metaphysics, embracing a Critical Analysis of Ideas, the Elements of Reasoning, and the Philosophy of the Feelings and Will," "adapted to academic and popular use." [117] Blakey characterizes the work quite aptly:

"This is an able work, though the writer does not appear to have a very extensive acquaintance with the history of philosophy. He lays down his positions, however, with great clearness; and his book must prove useful to general readers, and particularly to students." [118]

Henry P. Tappan,[119] later the first Chancellor of the University of Michigan (the old Catholepistemiad),[120] issued in three successive years three books on the Will, the first a "Review of Edwards," [121] the second "The Doctrine of the Will, determined by an Appeal to Consciousness," [122] and the last the application of his doctrine to "Moral Agency and Responsibility." [123] Although Brett consigns these works to oblivion, the Editor of the *British Quarterly Review*, while disapproving of some of Tappan's philosophical views as exhibited by his work on Logic,[124] says that his "work on the Will, abundantly shows his capability of contributing largely to the successful cultivation—to the real advancement of mental science, were he to limit his inquiries to psychology." [125] His pioneer work in university education diverted his attention to another field, however, in which he won great distinction.

The literature on the Will had been enriched during this period by at least three other books, "An Essay Concerning the Free Agency of Man, or the Powers and Faculties of the Human Mind," [126] by *Nathaniel Baylies* (1772-1847), and two by *Jeremiah Day* (1773-1867), President of Yale from 1817 to 1846—"An Inquiry Respecting the Self-Determining Power of the Will or Contingent Volition," [127] supporting Edwards, and "An Examination of Edwards." [128] Baylies "considers that the human mind has *two* powers, called the Understanding and the Will," but arrives at the conclusion that "the mind always wills with liberty or freedom." (pp. iii, iv.) Two quotations from Day are pertinent:

"Though President Edwards agrees with many European writers, in dividing the powers of the mind between the understanding and the will; yet he differs from most of them, in the wide extent which he gives to the latter faculty. They commonly confine it to *imperative acts;* leaving the emotions and passions, if any definite place is allowed them, to fall under the head of the understanding. His arrangement, which considers the emotions and passions as belonging to the will, is quite as rational as theirs. The mental states which he calls affections are as different from perception and knowledge as from imperative acts of will. The fact is, that each of these methods of classifying our faculties, is found to be defective. A *threefold* division of our mental powers is greatly needed, and, it is hoped, will soon prevail. Even then there will be occasion for a *subdivision* of each of the general heads." [129]

"Whatever classification of the mental powers we may think proper to adopt, it is of the utmost importance to bear steadily in mind, that distinct *faculties* are not distinct *agents*. They are different powers of one and the same agent. It is the *man* that perceives, and loves, and hates, and acts; not his understanding, or his heart, or his will, distinct from himself." [130]

Upham's little volume on "Disordered Mental Action" came out in 1840, the very year in which there appeared from the pen of *Frederick Rauch* [131] the first book in the English language to bear the title of "Psychology." [132] In Great Britain, in his annual lectures on Metaphysics, Sir William Hamilton was still laboring to prove to his auditors the convenience of the term psychology, patiently explaining that it had been used by such reputable writers as Principal Campbell, James Beattie, and Sir James Mackintosh, and that it was less cumbersome, especially in its adjectival form, than the phrase Philosophy of Mind.[133] But the obstinate British authors continued to muddle through with the good old phrase until Herbert Spencer published his "Principles of Psychology" in 1855, at which date the American book was already fifteen years old.

After an Introduction devoted to a discussion of the differences between man and the animal, and to the principle of life, including an interesting treatment of instinct, Rauch proceeds after the German fashion to divide his subject into Anthropology and Psychology.

"Mental philosophy has to consider the mind of man, 1. In its connection with the body, in its dependence upon it, and through it upon nature. 2. In its relation to itself. In the for-

mer case its doctrines may be embraced under the general term
ANTHROPOLOGY, and in the latter that of PSYCHOLOGY. The
object of Anthropology is to examine the external influences to
which the mind is subject, and its modifications produced by
them. The object of Psychology is to investigate the nature of
mind, as it is conscious of itself and of the differences between
it and nature, and as it has rendered these natural influences
more or less subject to its power. . .

"Anthropology may be divided into three parts: or those
which treat

   I. Of the *permanent* influence of nature, of race, sex, etc.,
      upon the mind;
  II. Of the *transient* influence of age, sleep, dreaming, etc.
 III. Of the power of the mind over the body." (pp. 53, 54.)

Every science has a central point, and in mental philosophy it is that of self-consciousness. (p. 176.) Various con
cepts of the relation of soul and body are discussed, and
the author develops his own view thus:

"It would be wrong to say, that man consists of two essentially different substances; of earth and the soul; but he is *soul
only*, and cannot be anything else. This soul, however, unfolds
itself externally in the *life* of the body, and internally in the life
of the mind. Twofold in its development, it is one in origin,
and the centre of this union is our personality." [134]

The distribution of the mental faculties is ingeniously
handled:

"Until recently, mental philosophers have been in the habit
of representing mind as a compound of many faculties, as a
whole made up of parts. . . This whole view has been
more or less relinquished, and one directly opposed to it has
been received. There is but *one* thinking power in man. It is

the same when it judges as when it observes, comprehends, thinks, or wills. The apparent difference is produced either by the object to which it is directed,—as for example it is designated as *memory* when directed to the past, *imagination* when turned to the future;—or, by the greater or less degree, in which it exerts itself. . . The mind is neither a multitude of faculties, nor is it a simple, identical activity, but it is a *union* that not only comprises the manifold, but produces it by unfolding its life organically. (pp. 192, 193, 197.)

"Psychology will be divided into two sections: the former treating of Reason in general, the latter of the Will. The section on Reason will be divided into three chapters. The

I. Treating on Sensation, or the *receptive* powers of Reason.

II. On conception in general, or the form-giving nature of Reason.

III. On pure Thinking. (p. 201.)

"It is usual to consider Reason and Will as wholly different activities, and to speak of mental and moral faculties. But the mind is one, and reason and will are so inseparable, that the one includes the other. . . *Reason is nothing else than will with prevailing consciousness, and will is reason with a prevailing practical tendency.*" (p. 293.)

The book is full of shrewd observations, thoughtful deductions, and stimulating suggestions. It was well received, the first edition being exhausted in a few weeks. But strangely enough its ultimate influence was slight, and it soon passed into an unfortunate oblivion, giving place to the more popular texts of Upham, Wayland, and Haven.

Samuel Simon Schmucker,[135] Professor of Christian Theology in the Theological Seminary at Gettysburg, published in 1842 a Psychology, which he called the "Elements of a New System of Mental Philosophy on the Basis of Consciousness and Common Sense." [136] In the true German spirit he evolved his system from the depths of his profound German mind, and like the good Lord, "surveyed everything that he had made, and behold, it was very good."

"About sixteen years ago, having been called to take charge of a theological seminary [the author] felt it a duty to devote particular attention to his instructions in this department, and formed a resolution, which has doubtless had some influence on this system. He had considerable acquaintance with the patriarchs of British metaphysics, Locke, Reid, Stewart, and Brown, as well as with some few German authors; but neither of them seemed to present an entirely natural and satisfactory exhibition of his own mental phenomena. He then resolved to study exclusively his own mind, and for ten years he read no book on this subject. During this period, he spent much of his time in the examination of his own mental phenomena, and having travelled over the whole ground, and employed the leisure of several additional years to review and mature his views, he now presents to the public the following outline of a system, as in all its parts the result of original, analytic induction. That he regards it as a more natural, faithful, and intelligible exhibition of the operations of his own mind than is contained in any other work which he has seen, he will not dissemble. Since the features of his own system have been settled, the writer has looked at various other works, and found much that is valuable, especially in the recent publications of his own countrymen, Professors Upham, Day, Tappan, and others, yet nothing which seemed to invalidate his system, or render dubious the propriety of its publication." (pp. vi-vii.)

He makes a threefold division of the operations of the mind into

I. Cognitive Ideas
II. Sentient Ideas
III. Active Operations.[137]

"They are all, in their own nature, either knowledge, or they are feeling, or they are action. . . The only method by which each individual can acquire a correct idea of the difference between these three kinds of ideas or mental phenomena, is by examining the testimony of his own consciousness.

"The first class embraces Perceptions, acts of Consciousness, Conceptions, Judgments, Recollections, the Results of Reasoning, but not the process, and the dictates or decisions of Conscience, which are nothing else than the results of our judgment concerning the propriety or impropriety of our own conduct.

"The second class embraces what are usually termed, first, Sensations; secondly, Emotions; thirdly, Affections; fourthly, Passions, to a certain extent. . . The third class embraces . . . Volitions, in which is comprehended the whole extent as well as every variety of the direct action of the will; the operations of the mind termed processes of reasoning, but not their results . . . the act of memorizing, and not its results . . . the intellectual act of communicating our thoughts to others . . . [and] some other active processes." (pp. 27, 28; 31-33; 36-37.)

The work excited favorable interest in this country, was noted by Beneke, and although without any trace of a permanent influence on the course of psychological development in America, received mention by Baldwin and Brett, the latter of whom manages to single out the least significant things in early American psychology for supercilious comment.

c. *Asa Mahan (1799-1889) and Laurens P.*
Hickok (1798-1888)

The German philosophy of Kant and Hegel was beginning to make itself felt in America, both directly and through the work of Cousin [138] and Coleridge.[139] More and more American students, following the lead of George Ticknor, were going to Germany to study in the great universities, and returning filled with enthusiasm for Kant, Hegel, and Schelling. German scholars like Rauch, Follen, Lieber, and many others, migrated to America, and brought with them their passion for metaphysics. A great Hegelian movement was born in St. Louis, associated with the name of W. T. Harris and H. C. Brokmeyer, and the *Journal of Speculative Philosophy* spread the gospel of Teutonic Romanticism. James Marsh's Preliminary Essay in the first American Edition of Coleridge's "Aids to Reflection" was a significant factor in the growth of a romantic philosophic movement in New England, centering in Ralph Waldo Emerson and the Concord School. Psychologically, all these backgrounds may be seen in the work of Mahan and Hickok, philosophical giants both.

Asa Mahan,[140] pioneer, preacher, college president, and philosopher, has left us in his "Abstract of a Course of Lectures on Mental and Moral Philosophy," [141] his "System of Intellectual Philosophy," [142] and a little volume on the "Will," [143] a psychological amalgam of Locke, Reid, Cousin, Coleridge, and Kant. He contributed to the demolition of the Edwardian determinism by concentrating his attack on the psychological argument and insisting on a threefold division of the faculties.

"To confound either of these distinct powers of the mind with either of the others, as has been done by several philosophers of eminence, in respect to the Will and Sensibility, is a capital error in mental science. . . We are now prepared to contemplate one of the great errors of Edwards in his immortal work on the Will—an error which we meet with in the commencement of that work, and which lays a broad foundation for the false conclusions subsequently found in it. *He has confounded the Will with the Sensibility*. . . His whole work is constructed without an appeal to Consciousness, the only proper and authoritative tribunal of appeal in the case."

His work added little or nothing to the body of psychological doctrine so ably enunciated by Upham, but contains many items of interest, especially in the insistence on the true method,[144] a study of the religious affections,[145] a "fundamental examination of false systems of philosophy, as developed in Materialism, and in the various forms of Idealism, as distinguished from the true system," [146] and a curious bit of evidence on the arrival of Sir William Hamilton in America.[147] His points are ably presented, and the Abstract especially, which was "printed but not published" for the convenience of his pupils at Oberlin, and at their expense, shows exceptional ability in developing, recapitulating, and driving home his topics with all the resources of a skilled teacher.

In the same year in which Mahan's work of the Will appeared, Alfred Taylor Bledsoe [148] added an important little volume to the literature of the subject. His "Examination of Edwards" contributed several important points to the controversy. The following quotations will illustrate:

"It is well known that Edwards confounds the sensitive part of our nature with the will, the susceptibility by which the mind feels with the power by which it acts. . . Now, the phenomena exhibited by these two faculties of the soul, the sensibility and the will, are entirely different from each other; and there is not the least shadow of evidence going to show that the faculties themselves are one and the same. . . It is in this confusion of things, in this *false psychology*, that he has laid the foundations of his system. (pp. 87, 127.)

"The hypothesis that the desires impel the will to act, is *inconsistent with observed facts*. If this hypothesis were true, the phenomena of volition would be very different from what they are. . . (p. 99.)

"Is the motion of body one and the same thing with the action of mind? They are frequently called by the same name. . . Let us look at these things just as they are in themselves. When a body moves, it simply passes from one place to another; and when the mind acts or chooses, it simply prefers one thing to another. Here, there is no real identity or sameness of nature. The body *suffers* a change; the mind itself *acts*. The one is pure passion or passiveness; the other is pure action; the very opposite of passivity. The one is a *suffering*, and the other is a *doing*. There are no two things in the whole range of nature, which are more perfectly and essentially distinct; and he who confounds them in his reasonings, as philosophers have so often done, can never arrive at a clear perception of the truth. . . *The analogies of matter can throw no light on the phenomena of mind.* (pp. 118-9.)

"Whether our volitions come to pass in the manner we call freely, or are brought to pass by the operation of necessary causes, is a question of fact, which should be *referred to the tribunal of consciousness*. . . It is to be regretted that President Edwards has said so little on this subject. . . Edwards did not observe the intellectual world just as it has been constructed by the Almighty, and narrowly watch its workings; he only reasoned about it and about it; and hence, he was necessarily compelled to go around, eternally, upon the treadmill of a purely dialectical philosophy, which of itself can yield no fruit, instead of going forth to the harvest upon the rich and boundless field of discovery. Why should the failure of other times, resulting from such a course, inspire us with despair? We hope for better results, not from better minds, but from better methods. . . How great soever, then, the failure of times past may have been, we should not despair. Nor should we listen, for a moment, to those who are ever ready to declare, that the great problem of the intellectual system of the universe is not within the reach of the human faculties." (pp. 224, 232-3, 234.)

Another great philosopher was Laurens Perseus Hickok,[149] "an original and powerful thinker, the ablest dialectician of his day." His "Empirical Psychology," [150] which made no significant advance beyond the positions taken by Upham and Rauch, was the textbook for many of the older generations of present-day American psychologists, but in his "Rational Psychology," [151] a ponderous tome of over 700 pages, we have "the first profound treatment of epistemology that had come from any American pen since Jonathan Edwards." [152] The first edition appeared in 1848, and the author realized that

"a few minds only of a generation turn themselves back upon consciousness itself, and reflect upon what and how experience must be. . . It is not expected that [this work] will be of interest to the many; sufficient quite, if it reach and occupy the minds of the few, and propagate its reciprocations of free thought through the growing number of such as can and do familiarize themselves in purely rational demonstrations." [153]

To his astonishment the work ran into a second edition in 1861, and the omission of some 200 pages reflects great

credit upon the college student, who, in the opinion of
the author, no longer needed the painstaking groundwork
that he had felt it necessary to lay in the first form of the
work.[154] In answer to a criticism of obscurity in his writing
he rejoins with some acrimony that "no words will put
thoughts over into the empty and passive mind." [155]

Empirical and Rational Psychology are thus distinguished:

"PSYCHOLOGY is the Science of Mind. *Empirical* Psychology
attains the facts of mind and arranges them in a system. The
elements are solely the facts given in experience, and the cri-
terion of their reality is the clear testimony of consciousness
. . . the general consciousness of mankind. What this general
consciousness is, may be attained . . . from the languages,
laws, manners and customs, proverbial sayings, literature and
history of the race. . . Such an appeal to general consciousness
may properly be termed the tribunal of Common Sense.

"*Rational* Psychology is a very different process for attaining to a Science of Mind. . . It is truly a transcendental philosophy inasmuch as it transcends experience, and goes up to
those necessary sources from which all possible experience must
originate. . . It enters into the very essence of Rational Psychology to make this apriori investigation of the human intellect; to attain the idea of intelligence, from the apriori conditions which make an intellectual agency possible, and thereby
determine how, if there be intelligence, it must be both in function and operation; and then find the facts which shall evince
that such intellectual agency is not only possible in void thought,
but is also actual being in reality." (pp. 17, 22, 23.)

Locke's theory of representative perception issues in a
twofold skepticism; on one side, Idealism, "which denies
all knowledge of the reality of objective being, save as it

exists in the sensations of the mind itself," on the other side, Materialism, "the doubting of all reality except that of material being." "There remains nothing other than to doubt universally." This Universal Skepticism of David Hume was apparently refuted by Reid, who, however, made an equally unwarrantable assumption, that the "human intellect was so made as to see the outer world immediately."

"Here, then, are two counter-assumptions standing one over against the other, nor can one demolish or be demolished by the other. . . One end to which the results attained in Rational Psychology may be effectually subservient, is the complete termination of this drawn battle, and the settlement of all these questions on the basis of an apriori demonstrated science." (p. 44.)

The *method* of Rational Psychology is succinctly stated:

"Mind is an agent, spontaneous in its activity, and puts forth its agency in three distinct capacities, the sentient, the intellectual, and the voluntary. . . The mind as one agent is competent for action in these three capacities. . . *It becomes necessary that we attain the subjective idea of each distinct faculty, and also the objective law of each, and the determination that they stand to each other as correlatives.* (pp. 107, 108-9.)

"In these conclusions of Rational Psychology, we shall find the data for demonstrating the valid being of the objects given through these intellectual faculties; and thus in each department we may also add the outlines of an Ontological Demonstration." (p. 110.)

In the following 600 pages of finely written, rigorously logical demonstration, Hickok pursues in turn the Sense, the Understanding, and the Reason, in their subjective idea and their objective law, bringing out what he calls both the colligation and the consilience of facts to prove the latter.

"This is then our remaining task in this First Part of our work, to find the law in the facts of the sense as correlative with our apriori Idea. The best and probably the most satisfactory method will be, to take our apriori idea, and for the present dismissing all regard to it as an apriori cognition, assume it only as hypothesis, and go out under its guidance to question the facts we may attain. This we will do in two ways. . . One, to assume the law as correlative of our idea, and with it go out and gather many facts which we may successively bind up in it, and which we may term the *Colligation of Facts*. The other, by taking apparently very distant and disconnected facts, and seeing how they leap unexpectedly within the law, and which we will term the *Consilience of Facts* . . The confidence in the general law thus deduced is augmented in proportion to the number of the facts and the distance whence they thus jump together within the same hypothesis." (pp. 235-6, 266.)

He manages to avoid the Scylla of Reid's naïve realism and the Charybdis of Kant's subjectivity.

"A philosophy exclusively based upon either the objective or the subjective is necessarily partial in its very beginning, and must eventuate, when carried to its legitimate issue, in one-sided and therefore erroneous conclusions. . . Let the *objective* be the starting point, and the observed facts in their law of experience must give direction to all investigation. . . We can know nothing beyond nature, we must conclude that there is nothing beyond nature to be known. . . An assumed God of nature must be nature still, evermore stretching the chain onward. . . Let, on the other hand, the *subjective* be the starting point. . . Such a philosophy has only to lift its eyes from its minute and critical examination of the goings-on of subjective thought within, and look out upon the bearings of its course, and it must find itself plunging into an abyss of abstractions empty and bottomless; from which there is no escape until itself, the soul, nature, and God are all lost together in an Idealism which ultimately vanishes in nihility. . . The only possible method of finding such a position (where science and skepticism may grapple in conflict) is from the final results of a Rational Psychology, which having given the laws of intelligence in the functions of the sense and the understanding, now completes its work in the attainment of the conditional laws of the faculty of the reason; and by knowing the reason in its law, may thus lay the foundation for demonstrating the valid being of the Soul in its liberty, and of God in his absolute Personality." (pp. 65, 66, 67, 85.)

Finally, his ontological demonstrations attempt to prove the validity of the phenomenal, the notional, the Soul, God, and the immortality of the Soul.

"Putting thus together all the facts of a comprehending agency . . . and finding in all that the only law is that of a free personality, and that without such compass of a personality in liberty no comprehending as fact is anywhere given, we have an induction sufficiently broad for deducing the general law of all comprehension; and this law in the facts is the precise correlate of the apriori idea of all comprehension, and thus gives science to the operation of reason. We have as demonstrative a science, for an intelligent *comprehension* of universal humanity and universal nature, as for the *conjunction* of phenomena into a nature of things, and for the *conjunction* of the diverse in quality into definite phenomena. We have thus the science of our entire intellectual being, including the functions of the Sense, the Understanding, and the Reason. This is all that we have proposed to ourselves, and in this we have a complete philosophy of the human mind—a *Rational Psychology*." (pp. 711-712.)

Rational Psychology is out of style in this age of experiment, statistics, and myopic behaviorism. Hickok did not intend it to supplant, but to supplement, Empirical Psychology. Some day, when the painstaking collection of data is reasonably complete, our psychologists will be compelled to make larger generalizations, and it may well be that Laurens Perseus Hickok will again come into his own. Meanwhile he is fair game for adventurous thinkers who yearn to get their intellectual teeth into some real food. The fare is tough, but it is good for the molars.

d. *Francis Wayland and Joseph Haven*

Three minor works need passing mention here. In 1852 Hubbard Winslow [156] published an "Intellectual Philosophy," a mine of citations of all the authorities in vogue at the time, including the recently issued "History of Modern Philosophy" by J. D. Morell, with which Winslow was greatly intrigued. In the same year as Winslow's text appeared Professor Alexander's [157] "Outlines of Moral Science," and in the following year, a "System of Moral Science" [158] from the pen of L. P. Hickok. All three books contributed towards the dissemination of the current introspective psychology.

Francis Wayland [159] (1796-1865), President of Brown University, author of a most popular text in "Moral and Political Science," and an exceptionally thoughtful and progressive educator, published in 1854 "The Elements of Intellectual Philosophy," "containing the substance of Lectures which, for several years, have been delivered in the classes in Brown University." Van Becelaere characterizes the work laconically as "plutôt un bon text-book qu'une théorie originale," and there is nothing more to be said. Wayland was anxious to make his work practical, and in a way anticipates the much later movement in educational psychology.

"It has been my desire to render this work an aid to mental improvement. For this purpose, I have added practical suggestions on the cultivation of the several faculties." (p. iv.)

All the early books are deficient in bibliographies, and the citations are often very difficult to place. Wayland varies the procedure by adding to each section

"references to a number of works of easy access, specifying the place in which the topics treated of were discussed." [160]

The work is strictly an intellectual philosophy, and as such does not go into the topics of the emotions or the will. It is well written, breathes on every page the kindly common sense and the educational acumen of the writer, and was well received and widely used.

The Professor of Mental and Moral Philosophy at Amherst College, Joseph Haven [161] (1816-1874), issued in 1857 a textbook of "Mental Philosophy," [162] the outgrowth of several years of practical teaching.[163] It is one of the great texts of the pre-experimental period, well organized, written in a clean, straightforward style, uncommonly free from the rhetorical flourishes characteristic of the period. It has an excellent bibliography,[164] and gives valuable historical sketches of the various theories of Sensation, Memory, Imagination, Realism and Nominalism, Logic, Aesthetics, Cause, Instinct, Sensibilities, and Freedom of the Will. The work is eclectic, but shows clearly the influence of Hamilton. In moot points it states the arguments on either side of the question, arrives at a definite position, and supports it by clear and cogent reasoning.

The general layout of the field of psychology according to Haven may be shown in tabular form:

I. The *Intellectual Faculties*
    1. The Presentative Power
       Sense, or Perception by the Sense
    2. The Representative Power
       (1) Memory
       (2) Imagination
    3. The Reflective Power
       (1) Generalization
       (2) Reasoning
    4. Intuitive Power
       (1) Primary Truths
       (2) Intuitive Conceptions (Space, Time, Identity, Cause, Ideas of the Beautiful, Ideas of the Right)

II. The *Sensibilities*
    1. Simple Emotions
       (1) Instinctive
       (2) Rational
    2. The Affections
       (1) Benevolent
       (2) Malevolent
    3. The Desires
       (1) Arising from the Physical Constitution
       (2) Arising from the Constitution of the Mind

III. The *Will*

As preliminary topics, Consciousness, Attention, and Conception are considered, and as supplementary topics, a chapter is appended on Comparative Psychology, as well as one on the Nervous System and Abnormal Psychology.

Summary

While the period from 1827 to 1861 reflected the Scottish Philosophy, tinctured as time went on by the eclecticism of Cousin, the transcendentalism of Kant, and the hazy romanticism of Coleridge, it was distinguished by the early adoption of the threefold division of the faculties, by the use of the term psychology, by the first systematic elementary text of Psychology in the English language, by the first systematic text in Abnormal Psychology, and by the manuals of Upham, Wayland, and Haven, to which there is nothing comparable in England before Sully's "Outlines," published twenty-seven years after Haven and fifty-seven years after Upham's first text.

The whole period comprised between the Revolution and the Civil War was most fruitful and productive. When an unprejudiced view is taken of the whole field of development, in America as well as in Europe, Johnson, Smith, Rush, Burton, Upham, and Hickok will receive the credit which has hitherto been denied them. They were by no means pale reflections of their contemporaries on the other side of the Atlantic. They made as real contributions to the science of psychology as James, Baldwin, Watson, and Thorndike have since made to the science which has taken its place, while still bearing its name.

CHAPTER THREE

THE PERIOD OF BRITISH AND GERMAN INFLUENCES

Progress of European Thought, 1861-1890

IN the short period of twenty-nine years from the outbreak of the Civil War to the publication of James' "Principles of Psychology," the world was growing smaller and drawing closer together through improved means of transportation and more rapid communication. America became increasingly more sensitive to the nuances of European thought.

In England, the Association Psychology reached its climax in the works of James Mill and his son, John Stuart Mill, giving way in general interest to the evolutionary philosophy of Darwin and Spencer. Galton began the study of individual differences, and Sully issued a series of modern and helpful textbooks. Taine and Ribot are the outstanding names in French psychology. In Germany, the work of Weber, Fechner, and Helmholtz in psycho-physics, Müller in physiology, and Wundt in physiological psychology dictated the momentous shift of emphasis in psychology from the study of the soul to the study of the brain and the nervous system. In America, the epoch-making work of William James, coincident with the return of the first Americans from Wundt's laboratory at Leipzig, marks the demise of philosophical psychology and the birth of a new science.

Conditions in America

In America, the population doubled between 1860 and 1890, moved further westward, changed still more significantly in ethnic character, and gravitated to the cities. The first five years of the period were completely taken up by the war, and a good part of the next ten was devoted to recovery. Living conditions changed greatly, but the acceleration of pace had not yet brought the vast changes of the twentieth century.

The religious picture changed again through the remarkable growth of the Roman Catholic Church, the rapid development of the Christian Science Movement, and above all by the coming of the Darwinian theory of evolution. The secularizing of religion went on apace until

"by the end of the century, evolution in a variety of linguistic patterns stretching from the defiant skepticism of Huxley to the genial Christian theories of Drummond had become thoroughly naturalized in the United States with widespread influence in every branch of mental activity." [1]

Educational development was checked in the North and practically annihilated in the South by the coming of the Civil War. The colleges were particularly affected. After the recovery however the number of colleges increased by 208, and then began to decline in importance until they were eventually overshadowed by the universities.[2] Men like Eliot, Gilman, White, Angell, and McCosh did much to change the ante-bellum college into the post-war university, modifying the form and intent of the institution, and making significant changes in the content of the curriculum as well as in educational procedure.[3] The new elective system foreshadowed the imminent discovery of the individual in education.[4] Wealthy men contributed huge sums to higher education, and as a result of such benefactions, university education expanded to an unprecedented extent and emancipated itself from theological control.

"Our colonial colleges were English in their traditions and curriculum. These modern modifications of methods and material have been German in their origin." [5]

American graduate students returned from the German universities with new standards of scholarship, and

"at last, American colleges and intellectual interests, as far as they were affected by collegiate discipline, felt the shock of critical inquiry and the impact of ideas wholly foreign to the heritage handed down by the theological education of the middle period." [6]

Meanwhile the college president ceased to be a teacher and became an administrator and a money-getter.[7] The old course in Moral Philosophy disintegrated for a time into a number of specialized courses,[8] one of which was Psychology, which was about to reform its methods, modify its aims, in fact, become a new science, without, however, changing its name, and enter upon a course of unprecedented development.

American Psychology, 1861-1890

During the brief span of the last period of Philosophical Psychology in America, Ray published a "Mental Hygiene," anticipating the spirit and many of the details of the twentieth-century movement, Hazard and Whedon made the final contributions to the swollen literature on the Freedom of the Will, and James Rush issued in two huge volumes a " 'Brief' Outline of an Analysis of the Human Intellect." Alden brought out a lucid little text which he characterized as "Elementary Exercises in Thinking," Bascom followed the lead of Hickok with a "Science of Mind," which emphasized the dynamic aspects of the intellect, the feelings and the will, and Noah Porter produced his massive volume on the "Human Intellect," "the most complete and exhaustive exhibition of the cognitive faculties to be found in our language, and, as far as we know, in any language." [9]

A series of minor publications led up to the dramatic production of the year 1886, the ultimate broadside of the expiring philosophical discipline, dogmatic and self-assertive in McCosh, vigorous but offensive in Bowne, systematic and idealistic in Dewey. All three works are reviewed in the first number of G. Stanley Hall's *American Journal of Psychology*, issued in November, 1887. The reviews continue with a hearty salute to the first important work of the "New Psychology." Ladd's "Elements of Physiological Psychology," over which Hall exclaims:

"It is at last possible to read a plain statement of the facts of a good part of the field of experimental psychology in English. . . As a whole, the work bears somewhat the same relation to the field it covers as President Porter's *Human Intellect* does to psychology from its standpoint."

In unmistakable language the *American Journal of Psychology* proclaimed: The king is dead—long live the king! The science of the soul has passed away with its mythical substratum. From now on we shall study the brain and nervous system, actions and reactions, reflex arcs and conditioned responses. Let the dead bury its dead!

The deceased revived the following year long enough to bequeath to posterity an excellent little textbook from the pen of David Jayne Hill.

a. *James Rush, 1786-1869*

Before attempting to evaluate the work of the younger Rush, three works which appeared during the War deserve some special attention. The first of these is a "Mental Hygiene," [10] by Dr. Isaac Ray,[11] Superintendent and Physician of the Butler Hospital for the Insane, and author of a luminous "Treatise on the Medical Jurisprudence of Insanity." On the title page is an apt quotation from Sir James Mackintosh:

"Health of mind, as well as of body, is not only productive in itself of a greater sum of enjoyment than arises from other sources, but is the only condition of our frame in which we are capable of receiving pleasure from without,"

and the foundation of all true mental hygiene is the principle

"that the manifestations of the mind and the organic condition of the brain are more or less conditioned by each other." (p. 2.)

"MENTAL HYGIENE may be defined as the art of preserving the health of the mind against all the incidents and influences calculated to deteriorate its qualities, impair its energies, or derange its movements. . . What we want—what, I believe, is within the range of the race—are healthy, vigorous, well-balanced minds." [12] (pp. 15, 17.)

It is recognized that mental imperfections are transmitted by heredity, that "mental deterioration is characterized by a strong proclivity to vice and crime," and that

"for the moral and intellectual elevation of the race, we are to look, not exclusively to education, but to whatever tends to improve the bodily constitution, and especially the qualities of the brain." (p. 22.)

The physical influences which affect mental hygiene are: the air we breathe, bodily exercise, diet, drink, sleep, and mental exercise.

"What is especially needed among us is a more prevalent and a more practical conviction of the importance of physical exercise as a habit of life. . . The radical fault in our modes of exercise is that they are unaccompanied by agreeable mental impressions." (pp. 75, 76.)

"The efficiency of the mind as a working power, will be affected, in a very great degree, by the stint of mental exercise to which it is subjected. . . A certain amount of mental activity is necessary in order to obtain the highest degree of mental health." (pp. 104, 106.)

Under the last head Ray makes an interesting study of educational practice from the point of view enunciated.

"The discipline of school, of obliging the tender child to sit upright on an uncomfortable seat, for several hours a day, and con his lessons from a book, is dangerous both to mind and body." (p. 136.)

In a chapter entitled Mental Hygiene as affected by Mental Conditions and Influences will be found discussions of most of the topics of the present-day science, often in twentieth-century terms: daydreaming, mental instability, tantrums in children, conditioned fears, the need for a well-integrated life with due attention to the proper use of leisure and well-motivated and steady work, a balanced relation between our abilities and our aspirations, and a consistent emphasis on the need for prevention as well as cure of mental aberration.

A thoughtful analysis of the practices of the times and a concluding chapter on the care of those who display tendencies to mental disease or who are already in its grip round out a discussion of a topic of modern psychology which in itself constitutes a vigorous refutation of the statement that there was no psychology in America prior to 1880.

The Reverend Daniel Denison Whedon [18] published his work on "The Freedom of the Will" in 1864, disagreeing fundamentally with Edwards.

"The method of Edwards was first to institute a psychological and logical investigation of the operations of the volitional faculty. . . We have first assumed the prior validity of the intuitions, and then sought by their guidance to ascertain how our psychology and logic may be brought into harmony with their dicta." (pp. 3, 4.)

He defines Will as "the power of the soul by which it is the conscious author of an intentional act," and Volition, as "that act of the mind which it performs with intention."

"When we say that the Will wills, we really mean that the entire soul, or self, wills. It is the man who wills, and his Will is simply his power of being able to will. And the free Will is really the man free in willing. As it is the man, the soul, the self, that perceives, feels, and thinks. The faculties are not so many divisions of the soul itself, but rather so many classes of the soul's operations, and the soul viewed as capable of being the subject of them. And as in volition the whole soul is the Will, and in thinking the whole soul is the intellect, it follows that the Will is intelligent, and the intelligence is volitional. When, therefore, we speak of Will, we speak not of a separate, blind, unintelligent agent, but of the whole intelligent soul engaged in and capable of volitional actions. It is in no way a separate substance or agent." (p. 22.)

He takes issue with Locke's thesis that uneasiness is the necessary antecedent of every volition (p. 43), and with the theory of Mackintosh, Upham, and others, that the volition must ever be preceded by an emotion of desire (p. 45).

"On the contrary, it is the clear decision of consciousness that the reasonableness or the intellective perception of advantage to one's self or another, or the perception of accordance with a previous purpose, or the intuitive perception of right, may so come in immediate contact with Will as to be the motive of volition." (pp. 44-45.)

In an interesting study of motives he brings out the incommensurability of "objects belonging to different denominations, or received by the mind through different senses, faculties, or impressibilities," and thereby finds a mode of attack on Edwards' determination of the will by the strongest motive.

"There is no commensuration or comparableness between a pound and a rod; between the brightness of the day and the force of magnetic attraction. Still less commensurable are material things with mental: as the weight of rock and the honor of a gentleman; the hardness of iron and the sternness of Cato; the length of a walk and the glory of a victory. It would not afford much sense to say that this night is as dark as this rose is odorous; that this timber is as solid as this woman is beautiful; that this fruit is as sweet as that crime is wicked; that this truth is as clear as that desire is strong; that this music is as sweet as that duty is binding; or that this color is as deep as that action is honorable. And yet these comparisons may represent the balance of opposite motives antecedent to volition. A cold intellection is not intrinsically commensurable with a deep emotion; nor a sentiment of taste with a feeling of moral obligation; nor a physical appetite with a sense of honor or duty. These influences receive their degree of prevalence, and consequently their comparative strength of motive, *from* the Will." (pp. 146-7.)

In discussing uniformities of volition as revealed by statistics, etc., he develops a sound psychology of Corporeal Nature, Disposition, Standard Purposes, and Habits, issuing in a theory of Character

"All human beings being *corporeal*, with a corporeity the same in nature, as if all were organic structures made from the same material, possess a still more specific ground of natural and necessary uniformity. . .

"By *dispositions* we mean the entire set of primitive prevolitional mental tendencies in the natural constitution, as well as all those that have grown, or been acquired, upon this constitutional basis.

"*Standard purposes* are volitions adopting an extended course of volitional actions, and to which, in consequence, an extended number of volitions subordinate themselves. They are plans, enterprises, resolutions, determinations, which contemplate and include a due number of volitions in obedience to themselves.

"*Habits* are uniformities of action which may be said to grow upon us by repetition. They are uniformities of volition, too; and they are often performed with so little deliberation as to acquire a resemblance to instinct. Positively, habit arises by the influence of the same recurring motives for which the Will will act. These motives are brought up by the laws of intellectual association of time, place, objects, and causation. Natural impulses seem to spring up in the being, physical and psychical, suggesting the usual volition. Meanwhile, negatively, counter motive and counter thought are gradually more perfectly and constantly excluded. No other than the given way is imagined or enters into the mind. And thus the volitions move, as in a passage walled upon either side. The wall is an amalgam of blending freedom and necessity. . .

"Thus, if we have rightly traced the process, is constituted *character*. Upon a basis of corporeal, physiological and mental nature, are overlaid a primary superstratum of dispositions blending the native and the volitional, and a secondary formation of generic purposes, wholly volitional, and formed by repetition into a tertiary of habits; and thus we have in his mingled constitution of necessitation and freedom an agent prepared for daily free responsible action." (pp. 164 ff., 165, 166, 168.)

Whedon's work was vigorous and constructive, but it was overshadowed by the masterly treatise issued in the same year by Rowland Gibson Hazard.[14] The author was a woolen manufacturer who wrote on boats and trains while on his business trips. His study of the Will was written at the suggestion of his friend, W. E. Channing, and bore the challenging title of "Freedom of the Mind in Willing, or Every Being that Wills a Creative First Cause." It attracted the favorable attention of John Stuart Mill, with whom the author entered into correspondence, and to whom he wrote "Two Letters on Causation and Freedom in Willing."[15]

Hazard's work is the last great utterance in the Freedom of the Will controversy. He anticipates a thesis of Thurstone that "wants are prerequisites of all intelligent activity," [16] discusses instincts and habit most interestingly, and develops his main argument in a series of propositions based on sound postulates. His psychological position may be summarized in his own words:

"Mind has feeling, knowledge, volition. . . Our sensations and emotions are not dependent upon the will. . . It appears that feeling, whether in sensation or emotion, is rather a property, or susceptibility, than a faculty of being. So also the ability to acquire knowledge is a capacity, or a sense, rather than a faculty. . . The mind has but one real faculty, or power to do something, and this faculty is designated by the term WILL.

"It is not unusual to speak of the will as a distinct entity, possessing and exercising certain powers. This produces much confusion in the argument on the 'freedom of the will.' It is obviously the *mind* that wills, as it is the mind that thinks; and we might with as much propriety speak of a thought, which thinks, as a will, that wills.

"WILL is the power, or faculty of the mind for effort. . . The mind has two very distinct spheres for the exercise of its activity—for its effort. In one it seeks to acquire knowledge; in the other it moulds the future. . . Every time a finite intelligence, by an act of will, forms a conception of thought, things, and circumstances, in new combinations, or in new relations; that is, every time, by effort, he conceives change in the phenomena within his finite sphere of knowledge, it is to him a new creation of his own, which, by other efforts, other exercise of will, other creations, he may, at least in some cases, make palpable or depict to other intelligences.

"The finite mind of man, made in the image of God, has finite powers corresponding to omnipotence, omnipresence, and other creative attributes of the Infinite; and, so far as we can know, exerts these powers in the same mode and under the same conditions; that is, it has wants, it has a faculty of effort, or will, by which to endeavor to gratify those wants; and it has knowledge, which enables it to form preconceptions of the future effect of those efforts, and to judge as to what effort to make, and thus determine that effort and the consequent effect, as in itself a CREATIVE FIRST CAUSE." (pp. 9, 10, 15; 24; 24, 25, 45; 49.)

In 1885 James Rush,[17] son of Benjamin Rush, published in two large volumes aggregating 930 pages a "Brief Outline of an Analysis of the Human Intellect, intended to rectify the Scholastic and Vulgar Perversions of the Natural Purpose, and Method of Thinking; by rejecting altogether the Theoretic Confusion, the Unmeaning Arrangement, and Indefinite Nomenclature of the Metaphysician." Brett sarcastically comments that

"before this trumpet blast the walls of philosophy might well have collapsed outright, but the teaching of James Rush was only a salutary infusion of physiology into the current theories which very slowly began to have a flavor of that 'materialistic' science."[18]

The younger Rush, like his distinguished father, was a vigorous and original genius. He began his studies on the mind in Edinburgh at precisely the moment when Dugald Stewart, in feeble health and afflicted by the death of a member of his family, delivered the Introductory Lecture of his Course, and then turned the remaining prelections over to his colleague, Dr. Thomas Brown. Two years later, disappointed in the results of his studies in mental philosophy in the very arcanum of the Scottish philosophy, he returned to America, and gave a lecture to one of his father's classes on the use of the mind in the study of medicine. His interest in the subject was aroused, and he recorded in his commonplace book his reflections up to the year 1823, when he became interested in the philosophy of the human voice, made a most exhaustive study of it, and published a huge volume on the subject.[19]

He laid aside his notes on the mind at the age of 36, and resumed his studies thirty-four years later, that is, at the age of 70. Meanwhile he had amassed a fortune of over a million dollars, which he bequeathed for the establishment and support of the Ridgeway Branch of the Philadelphia Public Library, adding a codicil in 1869, a month before his death, to the effect that the library should receive the copyright to all his works, but should engage to print an edition of 500 copies every ten years for fifty years, put them on sale at the cost of publication, and above all not change a word or even a sign of punctuation.[20]

"The original parts of them have been written *without assistance*, and I wish to be alone responsible for all the faults of thought, division, definition, and style, and of my corrected orthography, as I consider it."

The public response to his first work had been discouraging, and he wrote in the Preface to his magnum opus:

"Nearly forty years ago, the Author gave the magisterial pretenders to intelligence, fifty years, to comprehend the First, or Vocal part of his work. He finds, he mistook their capacity. On this Second Part, he will be more liberal: for as it uproots so many of the notions, habits, and prejudices of the narrow and stringent Lawgivers of Thought, he here allows them three hundred years, to clear away their piles of rubbish, and try to reconcile themselves jointly, both to the First part and to it." (I, p. 6.)

It is manifestly impossible to review this ponderous work in a few pages. It is diffuse and garrulous, but its main interest lies often in its rambling digressions. It is thoroughly materialistic, and lays an extraordinary emphasis on "the intimate tie between speech and thought."

"The mind as we only can know it; is an indivisible compound of Thought and Speech or other sign." (I, p. 4.)

It was no accident that Rush's studies on the mind were interrupted by a special study of the voice. He anticipated in an extraordinary manner the very modern concept of thought as sub-vocal speech. In another respect he is like the behaviorist of today in his hatred of the metaphysician. A master of invective, he rolls out sonorous periods against the arch-enemy metaphysics, "strictly considered synonymous with fiction," and fulminates with equal zeal and greater eloquence than his successor, John B. Watson, against

"the other mode of inquiry, if that can be called inquiry, which by waste of time, in conjecture and irritating controversy, produces nothing but a ground for further conjecture; and therefore not entitled to a scientific name . . . that notional method, we have already stigmatized as metaphysics." (I, p. 33.)

His system expressed in the briefest possible form is this:

"All that man perceives, thinks, pronounces, and performs is respectively through his senses, his brain, and his muscles. . . This fourfold human power, of perceiving, thinking, speaking and acting has received the general name of Mind. (I, p. 9.)

"The human mind is an effect of the organization of the senses and the brain. This mental function is governed by laws similar to those of other physical phenomena. . . Applying the term Perception, for these leading functions of both the senses and the brain [we] divide them into the following Five modes: PRIMARY, MEMORIAL, JOINT, CONCLUSIVE, and VERBAL PERCEPTIONS.

"These include the constituents both in state, and in action, of that part of the human frame, called the Mind. . . There are three great sources of human power: the Mind, to observe, compare, and conclude; the Voice, to inter-commune with the observations, comparisons, and conclusions of others; and the Hand, or other muscular agent, to execute the purposes of the mind and the voice." (I, pp. 41, 60.)

By an empirical induction he develops twenty-one classes of things, as the elementary materials of perception. The five constituent perceptions

"are practically exercised under varied conditions of form, force, degree, and other obvious changes. These variations, to whatever character, we call the *Qualities* of the constituents." (I, p. 42.)

The terms of the varied qualities of perception are eighteen in number, and the author devotes 175 pages to a justification of his extraordinary collection of attributes. The first volume concludes with a study of the disorderly and unproductive conditions of the mind, and a brief essay on the "sub-animal" mind. The concluding paragraph provides the transition to the second volume, which is to apply these principles to the analysis of human character.

"With this classification and outline, we are enabled more extensively to survey, and more definitely to name, the conditions of things and the characters of persons, than has been accomplished under the old metaphysical systems. Assisted then by the working frame and principles of perception, as far as here developed, we proceed to show, in the second volume, their application to the exact sciences, and to those subjects of thought and action, with their mingled truth and error, which occupy mankind; thereby affording a practical illustration of the ordained powers and purposes of the Human Intellect." (pp. 449-450.)

Rush ends the second volume with a "Brief Conclusive Recapitulation of the Whole Subject of this Work":

"We proposed, and believe we have executed; with whatever degree of success; an inquiry into the mind, as if it were a physical function of the physical senses and the brain. . . Having rejected the notion of immateriality, we no more suffered metaphysics, religion, popularity, conformity, or any other inapplicable motive, to interfere with our physical investigation. . . Hence our first proposition; that perception of images and types are material functions . . . our second proposition; that perception of the relationships of things is as truly a physical function as the perception of things themselves. . . We made five divisions of *perceptions,* and called them the constituents of mind: *primary* perception which is exercised by the senses; *memorial,* which holds in the brain, the images and types of things together, for the discovery of their relationships; *conclusive,* for determining the fact of their relationship: and the *verbal* sign or perception, by which the percipient communicates to others, the knowledge of what he perceives by the other four; which audible sign reacting on the mind through the ear, renders its images and types more vivid and durable; and thus the fifth constituent is like the other four, an essential part of the mind.

"We called the five forms of perception, the Constituents of the mind; for there can be no mind without them. But they vary in their power and efficacy. These variations were called their Qualities; and described under their eighteen different terms. The exercise of these five constituents, under their various qualities, was called the working plan of the human mind.

"Believing, then, the constituents and their qualities denote the whole of the intellect; we traced the differences of that intellect to the varied excellence, or perversion of its working plan: and endeavored briefly to apply the analytic system of perception, to the wide circuit of human character. We showed that all the variations of thinking and acting proceed from the five constituents, their eighteen qualities, and their various combinations with each other." (II, pp. 430-431, 432, 433.)

Behaviorism did not spring Minerva-like fully grown from the brain of J. B. Watson. It was announced half a century before by his John the Baptist, James Rush. If Mr. Brett got a chuckle out of the title alone without reading the book, one wonders what Harvey Wickham would have done with it. It would have furnished a magnificent chapter for his witty critique of "The Misbehaviorists." [21] In any event, Rush's monumental work is richly deserving of an extended section in a history of the development of American psychological thought.

b. *Noah Porter, 1811-1892*

Before attempting to analyze the "massive work on the 'Human Intellect' by Noah Porter, sometime President of Yale," with which Brett says the first era of American psychology ended,[22] two works of lesser magnitude may be briefly disposed of. The first is a bright little text, entitled "Elements of Intellectual Philosophy," by the Reverend Joseph Alden, D.D., LL.D.,[23] President of Jefferson College. It is dedicated to William Cullen Bryant, and was designed by the author "to aid the student in studying subjects which are adapted to promote fixedness of attention and discrimination of thought, and which underlie all thinking pertaining to human action and progress." (Preface, p. 9.)

The text leans rather heavily on Samuel Bailey and James McCosh,[24] takes a decided stand at times against the great Hamilton, and is distinguished throughout by clarity and common sense in the unphilosophical use of the term. It was cited by A. H. Strong in his "Systematic Theology,"[25] and stands out in an age of florid rhetoric and turgid philosophizing as the model of an elementary textbook.

John Bascom,[26] later President of the University of Wisconsin, published in 1869 his "Principles of Psychology," which he revised slightly and reissued in 1881 as the "Science of Mind." It may be characterized as "a strict exposition of rational psychology founded mainly on Hickok."[27]

Bascom proclaims himself an "unflinching adversary" of empirical psychology.[28] He acknowledges his indebtedness to Dr. Hickok, "the eminent explorer and instructor in this field,"[29] for the general tone of his philosophy, which he believes to have "the integrity of a system." He invites attention

"to the clear definition given to the doctrine of the intuitions; to the care with which they are enumerated, with which their relations to each other are pointed out, and their constructive office in thought is assigned them; to the development of higher powers in connection with lower ones; and to the support which liberty receives from the spontaneity of the intellect. Herein are secured a certainty of conviction, a strength of defense, and a clearness of explanation, not otherwise attainable.

The system lies in direct continuation of the Intuitive Philosophy." (p. vi.)

Of special significance are his chapters on the brain and nervous system, and his sections on the dynamics of the intellect, the feelings and the will.

"We are to speak in this chapter of the growth and interaction of the intellectual powers, of the dynamic states of the mind. The Intuitive Philosophy has been censured, not without reason, by the Sensualistic School for contemplating the mind only in its maturity, with no sufficient allowance for the results of previous conditions upon it,—for the effects of growth. This criticism we so far respect as to find a conspicuous place for truths which have been chiefly urged by such men as Spencer and Bain, always shaping them, however, to a new position and purpose. We are not prepared to admit any hereditary influences which vary the fundamental conditions of the problem of our intellectual nature. The varieties of character, the growth of national and race distinctions, find explanation here; but no sufficient proof has yet been given to establish, or even to render probable, the transformation of species by the accumulated changes of descent, with no increments of power. The past is not equivalent to the present. We must still regard each normal individual as the type of the race in its essential features; nor are we ready to look upon any one of these faculties as the product of simply external conditions, the sum of growing, hereditary tendencies." (p. 276.)

German physiology is appearing on the horizon, and new interests in genetic method and function are prophetic of future developments in American psychology.

The encyclopaedia of pre-experimental psychology, a vast compendium of the Scottish philosophy strongly influenced by contemporary German thought,[30] was the

"Human Intellect," [31] by Noah Porter,[32] President of Yale. Dismissed in a word by Riley and Townsend, it received the warm approval of Brett and the enthusiastic commendation of van Becelaere.

"German philosophy, diluted with dogma, was being taught . . . at Yale by Porter." [33]

"In this period there were few contributions to philosophical literature, but innumerable textbooks, outlines, and commentaries were published. Among the many teachers of philosophy during that time, some deserve to be remembered for the vigorous influence they exerted on the lives of young men, and hence on the academic tradition. . . There was . . . at Yale, Noah Porter. . . Although these men and their contemporaries were influenced in varying degrees by the German romantic philosophies, they were all definitely in the tradition of British philosophy. They used as textbooks such authors as Locke, Reid, Stewart, Brown, Paley, Butler, and Hamilton. They also prepared texts and commentaries of their own in that same tradition, and managed to establish Scottish realism firmly in America." [34]

"Published in 1868, the book breathes a spirit of concilation. It still retains the philosophic character of the eighteenth-century work, and comprehends psychological analysis, logical precepts, exhortation and metaphysics within the same covers. It exhibits an unusual respect for history, the afterglow of Hamilton's cosmic erudition; and is throughout a conscientious statement of the whole range of mental philosophy. The activism of the Herbartians seems to accord best with the author's religious presuppositions, and he gives the preference to such views as were, broadly speaking, 'spiritualistic.' But he rises much above the level of earlier theories, encumbered as they usually were with irrelevant theological or ethical purposes, and if the total result is somewhat vague in its eclecticism, that is due more to a lack of a definite co-ordination between the different aspects of the problem than to any vicious prejudices. As a critical compendium this book flourished for a quarter of a century, was separately printed in England as late as 1880, and is still known and quoted." [35]

"Caractère personnel, précision, documentation extensive et critique, tels sont les caractères de son premier et principal ouvrage. . . Son apparition fut un évènement d'une importance analogue, toutes proportions gardées, dans le milieu américain, à celle du traité de l'intelligence, par Taine, en France, et son autorité n'a pas cessé de se faire sentir. . . Outre son caractère personnel, l'Human Intellect représente un travail de spéculation intense et approfondie, au courant des derniers travaux de Mill, de Bain, Spencer, Herbart, Lotze, Fechner et Wundt, et empreint d'un esprit de recherche indépendante, mais toujours loyale et bienveillante à l'égard des personnes." [36]

The Introduction of some sixty pages is devoted to the definition and vindication of Psychology, "the science of the human soul," a discussion of the relations of the soul to matter, an inquiry into the question of the faculties, and an answer to the query as to whether psychology can be a science.

"While, then, psychology is an inductive science, with a peculiar subject-matter to which it points us continually, and to the source from which it is derived, as exempting it from the associations and prepossessions with which physical philosophy would invest it, it is not merely an inductive science, but is, in a certain sense, the science of induction itself. . . Psychology either furnishes or reveals the first principles for all those sciences which either directly or remotely relate to man." (pp. 52, 13.)

Van Becelaere states Porter's position very neatly, and also indicates his attitude towards physiological psychology:

"L'étude scientifique de l'intelligence humaine est, aux yeux de Porter, la base indispensable de toute saine philosophie. Elle doit être basée sur l'examen introspectif des faits de conscience, l'expérimentation physiologique ne pouvant nour fournir que des informations complêmentaires et subsididaires." [37]

The main body of the work is divided into four parts. Under the first head of *Presentative Knowledge* comes sense-perception, with a preliminary discussion of consciousness. Under the rubric *Representation* are treated Memory, Phantasy, and the Imagination, together with the Association of Ideas. The third section, *Thinking and Thought-Knowledge,* provides an exhaustive analysis and historical critique of logical concepts and processes, and the concluding section on *Intuition and Intuitive Knowledge* is ably summarized by van Becelaere as follows:

"Quant aux verites nécessaires ou intuitions il propose que les premiers principes ne nous sont ni donnés tout faits ni acquis par l'hérédité, mais évoqués dans l'esprit dans lequel ils sont nécessairement éveillés par l'experience, subjectifs dans leur source, objectifs dans leur cause excitatrice. Leur validité, contrairement à la conception kantienne, qui n'est pour Porter qu'une 'thèse' sans fondement, est certaine, et n'a nul besoin de l'échappatoire d'un impératif catégorique pour se vérifier. Les principes de causalité et de finalité, par example, auront donc une valeur absolue. La notion de l'Absolu, cause agente et pensante, n'est acquise ni par induction, ni par déduction, elle est impliquée par le processus inductif lequel suppose l'univers constitue selon ses forces et ses lois, par un principe inconditionné." [38]

After Porter's encyclopaedic work the numerous productions of the next twelve years seem puny indeed. At least twelve books appeared however. Bascom's work has already received mention. Of the remaining eleven some seem worthy of comment. The others will be taken from their dusty places in remote corners of the library, summarily treated in brief references, and then returned to their resting places to accumulate another half-century's dust, until another curious antiquarian appears to disturb their placid slumbers.

The texts of James Tift Champlin,[39] President of Waterville (now Colby) College, of the Rev. Oliver S. Munsell,[40] President of Illinois Wesleyan University (1857-75), and of William Dexter Wilson,[41] Professor of Philosophy at Cornell (1865-86), may be passed over in discreet silence. They illustrate Baldwin's comment that early American psychology was written by theologians or educators or both in the same person. The innuendo is not quite fair, because neither the one qualification nor the other nor their combination necessarily prevents the possessor thereof from writing a good psychology textbook. These *are* good textbooks. The material is well organized, and presented attractively with a keen sense for the teaching situation. The content is Scottish realism, and the psychology is content to be descriptive.

"The Physiology of the Soul and Instinct as Distinguished from Materialism, with Supplementary Demonstrations of the Divine Communication of the Creation and the Flood," [42] by Martyn Paine, A.M., M.D., LL.D.,[43] Professor in the Medical Department of the University of New York, author of numerous books, and member of many learned societies, naturally drew the fire of Brett, who seems to have been inspired to mirth at the bizarre titles of this work and that of James Rush, incidentally missing the significant contributions of early American psychology.

"Error was not the peculiar property of the philosophers, as may be seen by any one who reads the work of Martyn Paine, M.D. Beginning in 1849 with lectures on the Soul and Instinct, Paine was encouraged by success to enlarge this into a final treatise called Physiology of the Soul and Instinct (1872), which was to refute all materialism and establish finally the 'substantive existence of soul.' The author knew his ground thoroughly, and the work includes a great deal of (at that time) valuable exposition on the physiology of the nervous system and of operations due to the mind—e.g., nausea arising from disgust, contagious suggestion of yawning, and other points. The work as a whole was marred by the unfortunate and hazy conception of 'instinctive' action, a very transcendental operation which defies all attempts to connect it with the organism, and is a complete refutation of 'materialism.' " [44]

Brett's comment that "the work as a whole was marred by the unfortunate and hazy concept of 'instinctive' action" pales into insignificance beside the twentieth-century battle over "instincts," in the review of which Bernard lists over 300 books and articles on the topic,[45] most of them open to the same charge.

Paine's work on the physiological side was thorough and valuable. He sides with Professor Agassiz in opposition to the evolutionary theories, and in his way makes out a strong case against materialism. His interest in instinct was paralleled in a text by Paul Ansel Chadbourne,[46] successor of the famous Mark Hopkins as President of Williams College. As Murphy says:

"In accordance with the conception of man as a rational creature, a notion which had been kept alive especially by idealism and by the Scottish school, a contrast was frequently drawn between the instinctive behaviour of the brute and the reasoned conduct of man. Darwin (Descent of Man, 1871) had challenged this sharp distinction, and James urged (1890) that man actually had more instincts than any other mammal." [47]

In 1873 the Rev. D. Howland Hamilton, D.D., published an elaborate treatise entitled "Autology: an Inductive System of Mental Science whose Center is the Will and whose Completion is the Personality; a Vindication of the Manhood of Man, the Godhood of God, and the divine Authorship of Nature." [48] Psychology for Hamilton is still the handmaiden of theology.

Mark Hopkins,[49] President of Williams, one of the great teachers of all times, had been lecturing since 1830 and developing with blackboard illustrations his famous "Outline Study of Man,"[50] which was finally published in 1878 from stenographic reports. This book should be read together with his text in Ethics, "The Law of Love and Love as a Law, or Christian Ethics." [51]

He develops his system in a series of diagrams, which are worked out at the blackboard before the class, and which are all to be read from the bottom up. First Man is placed in the Universe of things: [52]

Man

Animal Life

Vegetable Life

C o h e s i o n

G r a v i t a t i o n

The principle of emergent evolution, strangely prophetic of the theory announced in 1928 by C. Lloyd Morgan, is thus stated by Hopkins:

"The principle is, that those forces, and forms of being, and faculties, and products, are lower, which are a condition for others that are conditioned upon them. . . At first we have only Gravitation, then Cohesion; but every particle that coheres also gravitates; then we have Chemical Affinity; but every particle united by that also coheres and gravitates, and so on upward till we reach man. In him we find at work Gravitation, Cohesion, Chemical Affinity, that Organic Life which belongs to the vegetable, a Life that is merely animal, and also that higher Rational, Moral, and Spiritual Life, which is peculiar to himself. *Everything is carried up, and then something is added*—it is not developed from what is below, or caused by it—but added to it till we reach man at the top. Man is there by the possession of everything that is below him, and something more—that something being that which makes him man.[53]

"We have now separated man from all other beings and things, and have found his place . . . now, in accordance with the law . . . we must make a further separation thus,—

Mind

B o d y

In our present state the body is the condition of the mind as we know it. We therefore place it below, and begin with the body. We wish to study man as a unity. This we can best do by a separation of the parts of his complex nature, by taking that part first which is lowest, and so a condition for all the rest, and so on upward till we reach that which is highest, and so the condition of nothing above it. If we can do this we shall have an 'Outline Study of Man' throughout." (pp. 26, 28-29.)

The systems that make up the body, their functioning and their products, are described and tabulated, and then the mind is taken up, and represented (reading from the bottom up as before):

Will
Sensibility
Intellect

"As philosophers universally regard it now, these are the general divisions of the manifestations of mind. . . For a rational being this is clearly the natural order. As rational, such a being can have feeling only as he has knowledge, and he can put forth choices and volitions only as he has both knowledge and feeling. This is the universal law, and this is the order." (p. 57.)

Each of these three divisions is taken up in turn. The Intellect is found to have a regulative and presentative faculty, a representative faculty, and an elaborative faculty; the regulative otherwise called reason or intuition, producing ideas of being, space, time, identity, number, and resemblance, while the presentative through sense-perception gives percepts and objects, and through the inner sense the ideas of thought, feeling and willing. The representative faculty through the association of ideas with its primary and secondary principles, fantasy, memory, both spontaneous and voluntary, and the imagination, produces dreams, air-castles, the past, art, poetry, and ideals. The elaborative faculty through comparison, abstraction, generalization, judgment, reason, and systematization, produces abstract ideas, the concept, a judgment, argument, truth, and system. This concludes the study of the Intellect.

"Hitherto we have considered the Intellect. We now pass to the *Sensibility*. But in so doing we do not leave the Intellect behind us. We take it with us. We combine it with the Sensibility as its condition, and thus find for it a new field, and get from both, as thus combined, new products." (p. 194.)

Intellect and Sensibility combined form the Affective or aesthetic Reason, and produce ideas of the good, the beautiful and the ludicrous. It operates through the *Appetites* (hunger, thirst, air, sleep, sex), *Instinct* (the various instincts), the *Desires* (for existence, property, knowledge, power, and esteem, resulting in concepts of the good, liberty, and society), and the *Natural Affections* (beneficent, defensive, and punitive).

"We have not yet found Man. . . . Thus far we have considered the body, and the two lower divisions of the mind, the Intellect and the Sensibility. These are indispensable conditions for the being and action of *The Rational Will*.

"Without the Intellect there is no light, without the Sensibilities there is no motive. As distinguished from mere impulse, rational will involves rational choice; but without the Intellect there can be no rationality, and without the Sensibility there can be nothing to choose. With these we have all that we need, not as a cause, but as a condition for the Will." (pp. 221-2.)

"By Will, or the Will, we do not mean anything that has a separate, or independent existence. We mean by it that constituent of man's being by which he is capable of free action, knowing himself to be this capable." (p. 223.)

Intellect, Sensibility and Will, working together, give personality, freedom, causation, rights, obligation, merit, demerit, responsibility, and punishment as necessary products. The grounds of action, appetites, desires, etc., result in the development of character (sensual, covetous, etc.). Conscience in its two phases of self-approbation and sense of guilt and remorse crowns the work.

"Conscience is our moral consciousness in connection with our choices. . . . In connection with these operations we have

Consciousness. . . In connection with moral operations we have also Conscience." (pp. 284, 308.)

In short, we have in this exhibition of American psychology before 1880, when there was nothing at all according to Cattell, an original and vital development of the theory of emergent evolution, and a vigorous conception of the well-integrated personality, both now regarded as "modern" points of view.

Henry Noble Day [54] and Aaron Schuyler [55] may be dismissed with a brief comment. Both were writers of school texts, the former having written nearly twenty textbooks on various subjects, and the latter several practical manuals. The work of Edward John Hamilton [56] is deserving of closer scrutiny. In 1883 he produced the "Human Mind," [57] reissued in simpler form in 1886 under the title of "Mental Science." Thirteen years later the title was again changed to "The Perceptionalist," the author's original choice, and republished as a University textbook. Hamilton was the author of several works on Logic and Ethics, and for his text on *The Moral Law* he was hailed as the "American Aristotle." [58] At an advanced age, wishing to have his books read in Germany, and unwilling to entrust them to a translator, he went abroad, resumed his study of German, and himself translated his works into that language.

Hamilton calls his philosophy Perceptionalism, and explains it thus:

"The word 'perception,' in its ordinary meaning and widest application, signifies the correct apprehension of fact or truth. On this basis, that philosophy which examines and explains perceptions as such, may be styled Perceptionalism. . . On the whole Perceptionalism appears to be the best designation for a philosophy which teaches that man's immediate or intuitive convictions are never mistaken, and that, under certain conditions and limitations, even his inferential conclusions may be relied upon." [59]

This is no dogmatic realism, but the result of a thorough analytic study of the operations of the intellect. In fact, the learned author criticizes Reid as "lacking in theoretic discrimination and construction," and the Intuitionalists, among whom

"no teacher has succeeded in founding a school in which like the patriarch, 'he will command his children after him.' . . We ascribe this to the narrowness and incompleteness of Intuitionalism. Correct, so far as it goes, it is but the commencement of a philosophy."

The Prefatory Dissertation presents a summary of Hamilton's epistemology, and the balance of the book surveys the whole range of the Intellect, to the neglect of the Affective Life and the Will. The author, after a critique of the classical distribution of the psychical powers, proposes a new enumeration into Sensation, or Sense; Thought, or Intellect; Emotion, or Sensibility; Desire, or Motivity; Exertion, or Conation; and the Capability of Pleasure and Pain.

"Each of these powers has characteristics of its own. For example, sense is distinguished by its peculiar and inherent dependence upon material excitants and bodily organs. Intellect is the most prominent faculty of spirit, and is the condition of all psychical life, save that of sense only. Emotion is a psychical excitement produced by the perception or thought of some object, and has a correspondence to the nature of the object.

Motivity is a more active principle than emotion, and is always a tendency towards some end. Exertion, or action, is an ability in the exercise of which the soul voluntarily uses the mental and physical powers at her command. And the capability of pleasure and pain is manifested in that peculiar experience, or element of experience, which, under laws of its own, accompanies all the different forms of psychical activity." (p. 19.)

The division of the Intellect requires three classifications:

I. First Classification (natural order of the operation of the powers)
   1. Primary
      Thought and Belief
   2. Secondary
      Attention, Acquisition, Association, Synthesis, Analysis, Abstraction, Generalization

II. Second Classification (mode of formation of mental states)
   1. Perceptive, or Presentational
   2. Reproductive, or Representational
   3. Discursive, or Rational

III. Third Classification (character of our convictions)
   1. Intuitional
   2. Experiential

Hamilton derives from the Scottish philosophy, but makes an advance upon it by constructive, original, independent thinking. It has been the fashion to represent our early psychology as taken bodily from Reid, Stewart, Brown, and Hamilton, either in the original texts, or in American editions or textbooks revamped from their Scottish originals. Van Becelaere states the case somewhat differently when he says:

"La plupart des auteurs qu'on rattache à cette école, ne doivent pas être regardés comme de purs *disciples* de Brown, Reid ou Hamilton. Ce furent des penseurs souvent indépendents. . ." [60]

The academic psychology of the early period had been content to be descriptive, at times venturing into the explanatory. It made no pretensions to be an applied science. Some of the earlier writers had made suggestions for the culture of the various faculties, especially Francis Wayland, who was much interested in the idea of an educational psychology. Meanwhile a literature was springing up for the guidance of the teacher in the schoolroom. Hall's "Lectures in Schoolkeeping," [61] Abbott's "The Teacher," [62] and David Page's "Theory and Practice of Teaching" [63] are examples of pioneer American works in this field. It was inevitable that the American genius for practical applications should sooner or later make use of the body of psychological data that was being accumulated and systematized. The Child Study Movement belongs to the story of the Transition, and Herbartianism reached us shortly after the date representing the close of this study. But in the last decade of the pre-experimental psychology, educational applications were being emphasized. In 1886 Louisa Parsons Hopkins published a little book of 96 pages, entitled "Educational Psychology," [64] a phrase that waited until 1903 [65] for a second use as the title of a book, and until 1911 [66] before a reviewer could exclaim, "At last we have a complete Educational Psychology."

The most striking work in this field before 1890 was "Mental Science and Mental Culture," by Edward

Brooks,[67] then Principal of the State Normal School at Millersville, Pennsylvania, and soon to become Superintendent of the Public Schools of Philadelphia. His text was "designed for the use of Normal Schools, Academies, and Private Students preparing to be Teachers."

Brooks' work is a textbook prepared by an experienced teacher.

"The special merit of the work is that it is suitable for a text-book upon the science. . . Every paragraph of this work has been written in view of the thought, How will this meet the demands of the recitation-room." (pp. 5-6.)

The author adopts the threefold classification of the faculties and adds,

"The first formally to announce this threefold classification of the mind into Intellect, Sensibilities, and Will, was Prof. Upham." (p. 27.)

But, like all the exponents of the so-called "faculty psychology" (a straw man set up by the moderns to knock down at their pleasure), he qualifies the divisions of the mind in the usual way:

"The mind, though possessing different faculties, is not to be regarded as complex. It is not made up of parts, but is rather single and one. It may act in various ways, and be regarded as possessing various capacities, but it is always the same thing acting under different forms, or in different ways. The mind is a spiritual unity, having many powers, but one essence." (pp. 28-29.)

The system in general is that of Sir William Hamilton, although the author ventures to differ from him in some particulars. It holds "that the mind is an entity distinct from matter . . . but does not ignore the physical basis of perception, and it thereby accepts one of the established facts of the materialistic school. But it rises above this school by assuming that the mind is an original source of truth, and that it can originate and comprehend necessary and universal principles. (p. 5.)

"The most striking feature of the work is the formal presentation of Methods of Cultivating the Different Faculties. . . To this part of the subject the author has devoted special labor, and having no previous treatment to guide him, his task was a difficult and embarrassing one. . . The discussions . . . may serve to awaken an interest in the subject, and incite others to a fuller and more suggestive treatment of the culture of the mind. (pp. 4, 5.)

"Education consists in developing the powers of man and furnishing his mind with knowledge. The act of developing the powers of man is expressed by the word *Culture;* the act of furnishing his mind with knowledge is called *Instruction.* . . To understand the work of education clearly the relation of Culture and Instruction should be clearly seen. The object of Culture is to quicken, strengthen, and enrich the mind; the object of Instruction is to furnish the mind with knowledge. . . Each of these two processes implies the other. . . These two divisions of education apply principally to that part of man's nature called the *Mind.* . . The one thing the teacher should know, whatever else he may not know, is the nature of the mind and the laws of its activity and growth. The object of the present work is to present this knowledge. Its aim is to give the student an idea of the faculties of the mind and the laws which govern their activities. In addition to this an attempt is made to show how these faculties can be awakened into activity, and thus trained and cultivated." (pp. 11-12.)

c. *John Dewey (1859-   ), James McCosh (1811-1894)*
and B. P. Bowne (1847-1910)

The old psychology went out in a blaze of glory. In 1886 James McCosh [68] published a two-volume work on "Psychology," vigorously and dogmatically affirming the basic principles of the Scottish school. In the same year Borden Parker Bowne [69] issued an "Introduction to Psychological Theory," in which he maintained that

"[psychological] knowledge is not possible by the way of physiology, and in any case the mental facts remain what they always were. Their likenesses and differences and essential nature would not be changed if physiology were supreme. . . Physiology remains a most estimable science, but the physiological reconstruction of psychology has been postponed." (p. vi.)

Alas for predictions! The very next year saw the publication of Ladd's "Physiological Psychology," [70] "the first and with its revision (1911) the most encyclopedic handbook on the subject in the English language." [71]

McCosh and Bowne were definitely of the old school. In the same year, 1886, there appeared from the youthful John Dewey,[72] a "Psychology," which seems to look Janus-like both forward and backward. Brett regards it as the definite proclamation of a new era, but G. Stanley Hall, reviewing all three books in the first issue of his new *American Journal of Psychology*,[73] asserts that

"Dr. Dewey's method is through and through speculative and psychology in its leading features is to him one of the most complete and finished sciences, instead of being in the most interesting stage of uncertainty and incompleteness. Not only all actual but all possible future facts are certain to take their place in this idealistic scheme. . . One who philosophizes by this method might exactly as well write a text book on any science whatever as on psychology. . . Dire will be the disappointment of those who hope to find in it the methods or results of modern scientific psychology. . . There are scores of formally quite novel definitions of nearly all the subject matter of psychology. . . Viewed from the standpoint of facts, very few of them are satisfactory, and many of them we believe to be fundamentally wrong and misleading. . . Besides definitions, the other ingredient of the book is illustrative facts. . . The facts are never allowed to speak out plainly for themselves or left to silence, but are always 'read into' the system which is far more important than they. . . In the field of these facts, the statements are extremely often vague, inexact and even mistaken. . . Omissions may be pardoned, inaccuracies never. . . The literary references at the end of the chapters will prove very helpful, but those of the most scientific value are not much utilized in the text, and nearly all these authors would not agree with the argument, for such it is, of the work."

It is likely that Mr. Brett read back into Dewey's first book the great influence that he later had upon the rapidly changing subject of psychology. Certainly Hall, who was an equally competent critic, felt that the work belonged with those of Bowne and McCosh, with which it was reviewed, and reserved a totally different reaction for Ladd's book, which he also criticizes in the same memorable issue.

The books themselves need not delay us long. They may be read today with interest and profit, and Hall's reviews should by all means be studied as the funeral oration of the old psychology and a ringing huzzah for the new. He pays McCosh and his new work a beautiful tribute and then proceeds to massacre them both. A few quotations will illustrate.

"The book is neither dull nor dry, but abounds in apt quotations in prose and poetry, stories, illustrations, sudden and unexpected but always impressive and hortatory passages, and seems to reflect, in the clearest and most direct way, the strong and beneficent personality of the author, not only his convictions, but even very many incidents from his own experience being interspersed. Almost every page contains taking points admirably presented to catch the wandering attention of listless students in non-elective classes. . .

"Judged from a scientific standpoint, however, little that is good can be said of the book. The wood-cuts of brain and sense-organs that are inserted are but little more related to the text than the marginal figures with which ancient missals were illuminated were wont to be. . . Many of the allusions to finer structures and processes by Dr. McCosh are inexcusably careless, to use no stronger terms. A still more grave defect of the book is the essential failure of the author to profit from both Greek and German philosophy. . . He pleads for the old Scotch 'realism,' as the ideal American philosophy. As the Scotch school may be said to represent hardheaded common sense, without the refinements or subtleties that are bred of specialized research, by any set method or direction, this is a most convenient attitude for a busy man, who must keep up the semblance of philosophy on short allowance of time and information, and must commend itself to many practical American minds who cultivate the power to make summary snap-judgments on all topics, finite or infinite. . . The book illustrates, in a word, not realism in any saving sense as the author claims, but eclecticism in every respect, which makes that word philosophically offensive."

Hall's critique of Bowne resembles the celebrated chapter in Shaw's Quintessence of Ibsenism, in which the author makes the critics ridiculous by heaping up without comment all the billingsgate that they lavished upon Ghosts at its first performance. Bowne does make spicy reading, and like James Beattie in his "Essay on Truth," he does not spare his opponents, and sheds both light and heat on the discussion. But Hall's review is equally stimulating. One quotation will illustrate a qualified appreciation together with the mildest of his remonstrances.

"The book of Prof. Bowne contains much current psychological matter and a few subtile criticisms. Though his spirit is much more narrow and provincial, the author is far better read in both the ideal and empirical literature of his topic than the writer of the book noticed above. But his work surpasses anything we have ever read in the field of modern psychology, not only in its hardihood of brunt [sic!] denial of accepted facts and interpretations, which if sustained would reduce many a settled consensus back to the plane of debate, but in offensive and ill-bred language, which can only tend to lower the controversy, and which fills us all along with painful doubts whether a self-respecting reviewer ought to touch it. . . The spirit animating this volume is utterly unlike that of Lotze, whom the author followed with such fidelity in an earlier work."

The year 1886 witnessed the final withdrawal of the psyche from psychology. McCosh begins dogmatically: "Psychology is the science of the soul." Bowne is a little more cautious. His first sentence is: "Psychology deals with mental facts and processes." But he does devote a chapter to the interaction of soul and body, and decides the question of the immortality of the soul by affirming that "the presumption must remain in favor of continued existence." [74] Dewey defines Psychology as "the Science of the Facts or Phenomena of Self," and restricts the subject-matter to the "facts of self or the phenomena of consciousness." He mentions the soul in a few unimportant passages, but definitely ignores its problem. Ladd considers Psychology "as that science which has for its primary subject of investigation all the phenomena of human consciousness, or of the sentient life of man." Hill revives the original definition for the last time in 1888, and James devotes a chapter to demonstrating the uselessness of the conception, summing up thus:

"My final conclusion, then, about the substantial Soul is that it explains nothing and guarantees nothing. . ." [75]

d. David Jayne Hill

The year 1886 marks the definite end of the old psychology. After the last expiring glow, a tiny but luminous flicker was emitted two years later by "The Elements of Psychology," a textbook by David Jayne Hill,[76] then President of the University of Rochester.

The text is the product of ten years' experience in the classroom, and displays the clear logic of a first-rate mind, and the organization and presentation of an experienced teacher. It abounds in historical notes of pertinency and value, and refers to all the standard literature, even including "Sully's Outlines," then only four years old. It has all the merits of Porter's abridgment of the "Human Intellect," which it resembles, but to which it is superior in clarity and attractiveness. It is a fitting valedictory to a scholarly period.

The old psychology had already raised many of the

issues on which the "new psychology" was to rear its pretentious but shaky edifice. Introspective methods were cautiously used, waiting only for a Titchener to introduce greater refinements. Induction of facts was the watchword, and an interest in the brain and nervous system was rising, although it was a moot question whether any quantity of information however exact in this field would ever solve problems that are essentially psychological. Abnormal psychology, mental hygiene, and educational applications were already a part of the subject. Quantitative and experimental research began in this last decade, although this is really a part of the history of the transition. The soul was still the subject-matter of psychology, inferred from its observable manifestations, and believed in on both logical and theological grounds. Whether the soul still exists today in a psychology which stoutly denies it raises an interesting question.

The shift from content of consciousness to function was less than a decade away, and this same John Dewey was to have a hand in making it. Within a quarter of a century the interest in physiology and a certain dissatisfaction with the practical results of the old psychology were to put the major emphasis on muscular and glandular responses, repudiating the aims, methods, categories, and terminology of the antecedent discipline. It is not too much to say that we have today a new and different science, a changeling, that continues to bear the name of its foster-father, but differs from it in every essential respect.

From the point of view of the new science, the contention that there was no psychology in America before James is correct, but, by the same token, there was no psychology in Europe before Wundt. If there is any value in elaborate, carefully documented histories of European psychology in the pre-scientific period, there is also justification for a similar treatment of the course of development on American soil. And in either case, what William T. Harris said in 1895 is still pertinent:

"All these contributions of the old psychology are of priceless value, as giving us the means to understand the place we occupy in the universe with our ideals of civilization. They furnish us directive power, they give us the regulative ideals of education, religion, jurisprudence, politics, and the general conduct of life."

If a revival of the Philosophy of Mind ever takes place, and psychologists with all the resources of the modern laboratory and experimental and quantitative methods, with the guiding methodology of evolutionary theory and the stimulating contributions of abnormal, comparative and social psychology, and the intensive study of the brain and nervous system, again face their research problems with the philosophical preparation of the old school and the giants of the transition, we may at last find the Galileo or the Lavoisier of Psychology, and our science may take its place with Physics and Chemistry, instead of being, as it is now, the battle ground of conflicting theories and crude though repudiated metaphysics. And it may well be, in such an event, that some of our neglected "early American psychologists" will be found to be weak indeed in scientific psychology as now conceived, but strong in philosophical insight into some of the most real and important problems of an empirical science, both introspective and behavioristic, founded upon a penetrating analysis of its fundamental assumptions and its relations to the whole field of human experience and knowledge.

NOTES

PREFACE

1. Cattell, J. M., *Science*, New Series, 1898, Vol. 8, p. 536. He repeats substantially the same witticism in 1929, *Science Monthly*, Feb., 1930, Vol. 30, p. 115.
2. Baldwin, J. M., "History of Psychology," N. Y., Putnam, 1913, 2 vols.

   Boring, E. G., "A History of Experimental Psychology," N. Y., Century, 1929, 699 pp. (Bibliographies and biographical data.)

   Brett, G. S., "A History of Psychology," London, Allen and Unwin, 1912, 1921, 3 vols. See Vol. III, pp. 255-261.

   Flugel, J. C., "A Hundred Years of Psychology, 1833-1933," N. Y., Macmillan, 1934, 384 pp. Good bibliography. See pp. 106-9.

   Klemm, O., "A History of Psychology," Wilm and Pintner, trans., N. Y., Scribner, 1914, 380 pp. See p. 139.

   Murphy, G., "An Historical Introduction to Modern Psychology," N. Y., Harcourt, Brace, 1929, 470 pp.

   Pillsbury, W. B., "The History of Psychology," N. Y., Norton, 1929, 326 pp. See pp. 235-7.
3. Baldwin, J. M., *Psychological Review*, 1894, Vol. I, pp. 363 ff. He makes no mention whatever of early American psychology in his "History of Psychology," *cit supra*.
4. Murphy, G., *op. cit.*, p. 181.
5. Curtis, M. M., "An Outline of Philosophy in America," *Western Reserve Bulletin*, April, 1896, 16 pp.

   Jones, A. L., "Early American Philosophers," Col. Univ. Contributions to Philosophy, Psychology and Education, Vol. II, No. 4, N. Y., Macmillan, 1898, 80 pp.

   van Becelaere, L., "La Philosophie en Amérique, Depuis les Origines jusqu'à nos Jours (1607-1900)," N. Y., Eclectic Pub. Co., 1904, 180 pp.

Riley, I. W., "American Philosophy, The Early Schools," N. Y., Dodd, Mead, 1907, 595 pp.
—— "American Thought, From Puritanism to Pragmatism," N. Y., Holt, 1915, 373 pp.
Townsend, H. G., "Philosophical Ideas in the United States," N. Y., American Book Co., 1934, 293 pp. (Good bibliography.)

6. Dewey, J., "Psychology," N. Y., Harper, 1886, p. 1.
7. Maher, Michael, S.J., "Psychology, Empirical and Rational," London, Longmans, Green, 1933 (Ninth Edition), 603 pp. P. vii, from the Preface to the Fourth Edition.
8. Heidbreder, E., "Seven Psychologies," N. Y., Century, 1933, 450 pp.
Ragsdale, C. E., "Modern Psychologies and Education," N. Y., Macmillan, 1932, 407 pp.
Woodworth, R. S., "Contemporary Schools of Psychology," N. Y., Ronald Press, 1931, 232 pp.

PROLOGUE

1. "The first author who gave a treatise on the subject under the title 'Psychology' is Otto Casmann, who in the year 1594 published at Hannau his very curious work, 'Psychologia Anthropologica, sive Animae Humanae Doctrina.' . . Subsequently, the term became the usual name of the science, and this chiefly through the authority of Wolff; Charles Bonnet, in his 'Essai de Psychologie,' familiarized the name in France." Sir William Hamilton, "Lectures on Metaphysics," Boston, Gould and Lincoln, 1859, 718 pp., pp. 95-6.
2. Schneider, H. W., "The Puritan Mind," N. Y., Holt, 1930, 301 pp.
3. N. M. Butler, in Schneider, op. cit., p. v.
4. Parrington, V. L., "The Colonial Mind," N. Y., Harcourt, Brace, 1927, 413 pp., p. 85.
5. Adams, J. T., "The Epic of America," Boston, Little Brown, 1932, 433 pp., pp. 59-60.
6. Eggleston, E., "The Transit of Civilization," N. Y., Appleton, 1900, 244 pp., pp. 2-3.

7. Tyler, M. C., "A History of American Literature," N. Y., Putnam, 1878, 2 vols., 292, 330 pp., Vol. I, p. 98.
8. Smith, Preserved, "A History of Modern Culture," N. Y., Holt, 2 vols., Vol. I, 1930, 672 pp., Vol. II, 1934, 703 pp., Vol. I, p. 38.
9. Sir William Hamilton, *op. cit.*, pp. 89-90.
10. Ebbinghaus, H., "Psychology (Abriss der Psychologie)," Leipzig, Veit, 1908; M. Meyer, trans., Boston, Heath, 1908, 215 pp., p. 3.
11. Schneider, H. W., and C. (Editors), "Samuel Johnson, His Career and Writings," N. Y., Columbia University Press, 1929, 4 vols., 526, 603, 641, 397 pp., Vol. II, v.

CHAPTER ONE

1. "At first all was wilderness, and had to be subdued. In that process the man with money found himself brought far nearer the level of the laborer than he had ever dreamed of being in Europe. . . There probably was not a gentleman of leisure on the continent, north of Mexico, unless he were a jailbird or a redskin." Adams, *op. cit.*, pp. 37, 46.
2. See Evans, "American Bibliography," Vol. I (1639-1729).
3. "Much used to be made of this event, but when we contrast the courses of study and the scholarship produced in our first 'college' with what the Spaniards had achieved long before at such universities as those in Mexico or Lima, perhaps a more modest estimate of this event in our educational history may be preferable. It tended, moreover, to increase the provincialism of New England by encouraging it to keep students at home for an inferior training instead of sending them, as the other colonists later did, to enjoy the better opportunities of Europe." Adams, J. T., "History of the United States," Vol. I, N. Y., 1932, Scribner, 306 pp., p. 41.
4. Tyler, *op. cit.*, I, p. 88.
5. In 1702 the first student presented himself for instruction, and by 1716, 56 students had been graduated, and a dozen pupils moved to New Haven, leaving about a dozen more at Weth-

ersfield, and three or four at Saybrook. For details, see
Dexter, F. B., "Sketch of the History of Yale University,"
N. Y., Holt, 1887, 108 pp., pp. 7-20.

6. "Autobiography of Samuel Johnson," in Schneider, *op cit.*, I,
5-6 (italics mine).

7. Samuel Johnson, 1696-1772. Born at Guilford, Conn. Entered
Yale (then the Collegiate School at Saybrook) at the age of
14. In 1716, the College was moved to New Haven, and
Johnson became a tutor. Left in 1719, and the next year
took a Congregational pastorate at West Haven "to be near
the college." In 1722 went to England and received holy
orders in the Anglican Church. In 1724 became the first
Connecticut clergyman of that faith. Was the friend and
correspondent of Berkeley during the latter's residence in
America (1729-31), and is probably the Crito of the "Minute Philosopher," which was written in Rhode Island. In
1743, received the degree of D.D. from Oxford. Resigned
his pastorate to become the first president of King's College
(1754-63).

Published in 1731 a small tract entitled "An Introduction
to the Study of Philosophy," in 1746, "A System of Morality," and in 1752, the "Elementa Philosophica" (B. Franklin, Printer). The London edition of 1754 has an Editor's
Preface by Will Smith, first Provost of the University of
Pennsylvania.

"Autobiography" in Schneider, I, pp. 3-49; see also *ibid.*,
II, pp. 52-70. "Dictionary of American Biography;"
Sprague's "Annals of the American Pulpit"; Chandler,
T. B., "Life of Samuel Johnson," N. Y., Swords, 1824, 209
pp.; Beardsley, E. E., "Life and Correspondence of Samuel
Johnson," N. Y., Hurd and Houghton, 1873, 380 pp.;
Schneider, *op. cit.*, and discussed in Jones, pp. 22-45; Riley,
"American Philosophy," Ch. II, pp. 63-125; Riley, "Ameri-
can Thought," pp. 19-28; Townsend, pp. 25-32.

8. Schneider, *op. cit.*, II, p. 186.

9. "Physica agit de iis rebus quae nascuntur et producuntur non
arte sed natura." These first points are quoted from the

"Synopsis Philosophiae Naturalis," a manuscript probably dating from 1714 (Schneider, II, p. 24), and given in Latin on the even pages of Schneider, II, pp. 24-52.

10. This naïve history of philosophy is abridged from the opening sections of the "Ars Encyclopaidia," 1714, given in Latin on the even pages of pp. 58-186 in Schneider, Vol. II.

11. In the Synopsis the question and answer form is used. The following will scrve as an example:

Q(uaestio)   67. "Quid est Spiritus?
R(esponsum)   Spiritus est Natura Constans, vivens et intelligens.
Q.   68. Quotuplex est Spiritus?
R.   Spiritus duplex est viz. Angelus et Anima rationalis. Sed propter unionem cum Corpore Anima rationalis in homine demum consideratur."

12. The rest of the analysis of Johnson's thought is taken from the Encyclopaedia, which consists of numbered propositions, of which the following are illustrations:

807. Spiritus est natura vivens, intelligens, ac volens.
808. Ejus sunt facultates et species.
809. Facultates sunt vita, intellectus, et voluntas.

The text paraphrases Propositions 807-814; 897-998.

13. Propositions 997-998.

14. Adams, J. T., "Provincial Society," N. Y., Macmillan, 1927, 374 pp., p. 279.

15. N. M. Butler, in Schneider, I, vi. Princeton, 1746, Pennsylvania, 1753, King's, 1754.

16. William Brattle, 1662-1717. Born in Boston. Graduated from Harvard in 1680, and was tutor for about ten years (c. 1686-96). While President Increase Mather was in England, Brattle was practically at the head of the College, but was forced to leave on account of his liberalism. In 1696, became pastor of the church in Cambridge, where he remained until his death. He and his brother Thomas figure largely in the liberal movement in New England Theology.

"Dictionary of American Biography;" Sprague, "Annals

of the American Pulpit." Discussed in Jones, pp. 10-12; Townsend, pp. 24-25.

17. Eggleston, *op. cit.*, p. 246. See also Rand, "Philosophical Instruction in Harvard from 1636 to 1906," *Harvard Grad. Mag.*, Vol. 37, 1928-29, pp. 29-47.

18. Ramus, 1515-1572 (killed in the massacre of St. Bartholomew). See Mansel, "Artis Logicae Rudimenta," xliii; Bayne, "Port Royal Logic," xxv ff., pp. 376-8. In 1672, John Milton published a little work entitled "Artis Logicae Plenior Institutio ad Petri Rami Methodum Concinnata," in Works, Vol. 11, N. Y., Col. Univ. Press, 1935. "Of the older writers on Logic in Latin, the one I would principally recommend to you is Burgersdyk—Burgersdicius." Sir W. Hamilton, "Logic," Lecture IV, p. 51.

19. Mass. Hist. Soc. Coll., Vol. II, p. 115. "In the earlier years of the college each student was accustomed to transcribe for himself certain treatises in manuscript on logic and other studies made by Alexander Richardson of Oxford." Letter of Leonard Hoar, Mass. Hist. Coll., Vol. VI, in Eggleston, *op. cit.*, p. 248.

20. 1735, several times reprinted, used as a text at Harvard (in printed form) from 1735-65. Evans, "American Bibliography." See also Peirce, B., "History of Harvard University," Cambridge, Brown, Shattuck, 1833, 316 pp., and Appendix, 159 pp., p. 91. Copy in Harvard Library (Boston, Draper, 1758).

About Descartes' "Logic," Mansel, *op. cit.*, xlv, says: "The Regulae ad directionem ingenii, a posthumous work of Descartes, is sometimes called his Logic. . . This work, though fuller, is in principle the same as the Discours de la Methode. . . To call the Discours . . . a treatise on Logic, is simply to assume for the Aristotelian Logic a purpose never contemplated by Aristotle or his followers, and then to classify under the same head works pursuing this supposed end by totally different means."

21. Townsend, *op. cit.*, p. 24.

22. Jones, *op. cit.*, p. 11. A few direct quotations from Brattle will illustrate:

Page 1. Q. *Quid est Logica?*
R. Logica est Ars Cogitandi; seu Ars Utendi
nostra Ratione in comparanda Cognitione.
Q. *Quid intendit haecce vox COGITANDI?*
R. Intendit quattuor * Operationes Mentis, scil.
Apprensionem, Judicium, Discursum, et
Dispositionem.

* *Cogitationes* sive *dicuntur operationes,* i.e. actiones *mentis,* sive
modificationes (et ita passiones) *mentis, eodem recidit* in Logica;
etiamsi non in metaphysica.

Page 2. Q. *Quid est perceptio, seu Apprehensio?*
R. Perceptio est nuda et simplex Rerum, quae
menti sistuntur, Contemplatio.
Page 8. Q. *Quando dicitur Mens sentire?*
R. Cum Objecta sensibilia praesentia sunt et
Organa exteriora afficiunt.

23. See Schneider, II, pp. 6-7. For the Encyclopaedia, *ibid.*, pp.
201-216, and for the Logic, *ibid.*, pp. 217-243.
24. From the "Revised Encyclopaedia," Schneider, II, p. 213
25. This is an early attempt to give a name to psychology and
define its field.
26. From the "Logic," Schneider, II, pp. 219 ff.; italics mine and
punctuation somewhat revised.
27. "Works of President Edwards," S. E. Dwight, ed., Vol. I, pp.
34-40; complete in the Appendix, I, pp. 664-702.
28. On the controversy as to whether Edwards had read Berkeley
or came independently to his conclusions, see Allen, A. V. G.,
"Jonathan Edwards," Boston, Houghton Mifflin, 1889, 401
pp., pp. 14 ff.; Lyon, G., "L'Idéalisme en Angleterre au
XVIIIe Siècle," Paris, Alcan, 481 pp., pp. 371-405.
29. Note by S. E. Dwight, in "Works," I, 702.
30. *Ibid.*, I, p. 40.
31. In Schneider, I., pp. 497-526, there is a list "of Books read
by me from year to year since I left Yale College, i.e., after
I was Tutor of the College."
32. Berkeley was in America from February, 1729, until Septem-
ber, 1731. See Johnson's Autobiography in Schneider, I.,

pp. 24-27. Johnson had already read the "Principles of Human Knowledge," and now met the Bishop and had considerable correspondence with him (reproduced in full in Schneider, II, pp. 261-284). See also Riley, "American Thought," pp. 19-28, especially pp. 19-22; Jones, pp. 22-45, especially pp. 23-24; Townsend, pp. 25-32, especially pp. 26, 28.

33. Schneider, II, p. 358. The full title is "Elementa Philosophica / Containing chiefly / NOETICA / Or Things relating to the / Mind or Understanding: / and / ETHICA / Or Things relating to the / Moral Behavior." Published in Philadelphia in 1752 by Benjamin Franklin. Copies at Columbia and Yale. Reproduced in full in Schneider, Vol. II, pp. 359-518, together with a Section, pp. 307-356, entitled "The Growth of Samuel Johnson's Introduction to Philosophy," most useful for tracing the genesis of the work. Discussed in Riley, Jones, Townsend, etc.

34. Baldwin, J. M., editor, "Dictionary of Philosophy and Psychology," N. Y., Macmillan, 1901, New Edition, 1911, 4 vols. in 3.

35. From "An Outline of Philosophy," 1730, in Schneider, II, p. 311.

36. Synopsis of Philosophy, in "An English and Hebrew Grammar," 1771, Schneider, II, pp. 355-6. See also "El. Phil.," Introduction, Sec. 13, in Schneider, II, p. 366.

37. "El. Phil.," Noetica, Ch. I, Sec. 2, in Schneider, II, pp. 372-3.

38. Schneider, II, pp. 372, 364.

39. Ethica, Ch. III, Sec. 21, in Schneider, II, pp. 483-4.

40. Schneider, II, pp. 317-8.

41. Hartley was publishing his "Observations on Man" in 1749. This Bibliography dates from about 1744.

42. This and the following extracts are from Schneider, Vol. II.

43. "El. Phil." in Schneider, II, p. 451. See also pp. 460, 474, 493, 507; also Vol. III, *passim*, especially pp. 576 ff.

44. E.g., moral education, proper use of praise and blame, p. 425; nature study, p. 426; study of geography and institutions beginning with immediate surroundings, p. 427; music, p. 428; practical problems, p. 429; science teaching, p. 431;

social science, p. 433; gradation of studies, p. 362; history, p. 362; use of maps, globes and other apparatus, p. 362 *et passim*, etc., etc.

45. Jones, *op. cit.*, p. 45.
46. "El. Phil.," in Schneider, II, p. 458. See also p. 497.
47. Jonathan Edwards, 1703-1758. Born in East Windsor, Conn. Entered Yale in 1716, coming into contact with Locke the following year. Graduated in 1720, remaining for two years as resident graduate. After a brief experience in the pulpit, returned to Yale in 1724 as Tutor. In 1727, became assistant to his grandfather, Solomon Stoddard, pastor of the church at Northampton, being chosen sole pastor at the death of the latter in 1729. In 1734 and 1735 there was a great religious revival in the church, returning again in 1740 as the "Great Awakening," during which Edwards preached the famous sermon, "Sinners in the Hands of an Angry God." In 1750 he was dismissed, going the following year to Stockbridge as missionary to the Indians. In 1758 he was called to the Presidency of the College of New Jersey, where he took up his duties in February, and died in March of an inoculation against the smallpox. His writings include a "Treatise on the Religious Affections," 1746, "Enquiry into the Freedom of the Will," 1754, "Treatise on the Nature of True Virtue," 1755, and "God's End in the Creation of the World," 1758 (the last two published posthumously in 1788).

"Works" in ten volumes, edited by S. E. Dwight, the first volume including the most extensive biographical study we have, together with the Notes on Mind, on Natural Science, etc. See also Sprague, "Annals of the American Pulpit"; Allen, "Jonathan Edwards," with bibliography, especially pp. 381-401; Parks, "Jonathan Edwards, the Fiery Puritan"; "Dictionary of American Biography."

Discussed by Jones, pp. 46-78, especially pp. 49-55; Townsend, pp. 35-62, especially pp. 40-45; Riley, "American Thought," pp. 28-36; Riley, "American Philosophy," pp. 126-187; Parrington, "The Colonial Mind," Vol. I, pp. 148-164; Blakey, "History of the Philosophy of Mind,"

Vol. IV, pp. 492-519; Tappan, "Review of Edwards," pp. 15-86; summary in pp. 72-85, comparison with Locke, pp. 85-86; Foster, F. H., "A Genetic History of the New England Theology," Chicago, U. of Chi. Press, 1907, 586 pp., pp. 47-103, especially pp. 62-81.

48. Parrington, "The Colonial Mind," pp. 149, 151.

49. The problem of free-will is raised by Plato in the Republic, Book X, and by Aristotle in Book III of the Ethics *et passim*. The Stoics were determinists, but Chrysippus attempted to reconcile determinism with moral responsibility; the Epicurians inclined to a belief in free-will. "Christianity, from the beginning, was faced with the problem of reconciling human freedom with divine government—the old Stoic problem in fact" (A. Wolf, in the Encyclopaedia Britannica, 14th Ed., Article, Free Will). St. Augustine inclined to free-will, followed in the main by Thomas Aquinas. Hobbes was a thoroughgoing determinist, Descartes however allowed to the will the power of self-determination. Locke ridiculed the idea of the "freedom of the will," and substituted the expression "freedom of the man" to will or not to will, supporting freedom in this corrected form (Book II, Ch. 21). This brings the controversy down to Edwards, who was familiar with Locke. See the article in the Encyclopaedia Britannica, 14th Ed., and a more elaborate article in the 11th Ed. See also Stewart, "Active and Moral Powers of Man," Walker's Ed., Boston, 1855, pp. 268-324 (originally an appendix).

The controversy in America after Edwards was carried on by a number of writers, including Day, Dana, Whedon, Tappan, Hazard, and Bledsoe (*vide infra*). It has never been settled. While modern science rests upon a conception of cause and effect that makes every action grow out of antecedent causes in such a way that man is absolutely determined, biology and psychology assume a certain spontaneity in the living organism that inclines to freedom within limits. See Dampier-Whetham, W. C. D., "A History of Science," N. Y., Macmillan, 1930, 514 pp., pp. 471-477.

50. The metaphysical arguments may be summed up thus: "Everything must have a cause, acts of the will included; to say that man has free will is to say that he is free to choose what he chooses, which is absurd. The argument is irrefutable, but as Edwards expressly identifies the will with the emotions, it remains rather a tour de force" (Park, p. 241). Allen says (p. 289): "Edwards' argument against the freedom of the human will, in the sense of a power to choose between good and evil, gains its force from the assumption of the thing to be proved. There is no movement in his thought beyond this assumption that every event must have some external cause." Thus the metaphysical argument rests upon the concept of causality.

The theological argument is based upon the omniscience of God, supported by elaborate quotation of Bible passages (weak philosophically, the divine inspiration of the Scriptures being taken for granted). For a man to be able to do anything that God does not foresee would be to weaken the concept of the Deity. If God foresees every action, it is necessarily determined.

Edwards' argumentation was so cogent that even Hazard admitted that "almost by common consent, his positions are deemed impregnable, and the hope of subverting them by direct attack abandoned" (p. 173, Ed. of 1865). Another writer says (quoted by Allen, p. 286): "Nibbling about the points of his arguments there certainly has been, but for the most part it has been extremely chary; and we suspect that the few who have taken hold in earnest have in the end found pretty good reason to repent of their temerity."

The psychological argument was refuted by H. P. Tappan in 1839. Vide infra.

51. "We see that the living creature is moved by intellect, imagination, purpose, wish and appetite. And all of these are reducible to *Mind* and *Desire*." Aristotle, "De Motu Animalium," Sec. 6.

"The vulgar division of the faculties, adopted by Reid, into those of the *Understanding* and those of the *Will*, is to be traced to the classification, taken in the Aristotelian school, of the powers into *gnostic*, or cognitive, and *orectic*, or appetent." Hamilton, "Reid's Works," I, p. 242.

"His [Aristotle's] is a faculty psychology, but not in the sense that he evades the task of the genuine explanation of facts by referring it to a mystical faculty of doing this or doing that. He is simply taking account of the fact that the soul does exhibit a variety of operations, and that behind each of these intermittent operations we must suppose a power of operating. But these faculties do not coexist like stones in a heap." Ross, W. D., "Aristotle," London, Methuen, 1923, 300 pp., p. 133.

"By a faculty is meant the mind's capability of undergoing a particular kind of activity. . . These activities assume either of two generically different forms. Every mental act or energy constitutes a relation between the mind or subject and the object or terminus of that act. Now this relation we find always to consist either in (a) the assumption by the soul of the object into itself after a psychical manner (imagine intentionali), or (b) the tendency of the soul towards or from the object as the latter is in itself. In the previous case the object of the state is presented in the mind by a *cognitive* act, in the latter the mind is inclined towards or from the object by an *appetitive* act. . . Under the faculty of cognition or knowledge are aggregated such operations as those of sense-perception, memory, imagination, judgment, and reasoning; under the affective or appetitive faculty are included desires, aversions, emotions, volitions, and the like." Maher, *op. cit.*, pp. 29-30. This is a clear statement in modern terms of the Aristotelian and Thomistic position. Father Maher argues that the tri-partite division sins by excess and defect, asserting without sufficient grounds the existence of a separate third faculty (p. 35). "Feelings understood as emotional states are, we believe, not the off-spring of a third ultimately distinct energy, but complex products arising from the combination of cognitive and appetitive activities" (p. 41).

52. Edwards, "Nature of the Affections," Part I. . . "Revival of Religion in New England," Part I.

53. "Review of Edwards," pp. 72-73.
54. "Freedom of the Will," Part I, Sec. I.
55. *Ibid.*
56. *Ibid.*, Sec. 2; Part III, Sec. 7; Part I, Sec. 2.
57. "This division of the phenomena of mind into the three great classes of the Cognitive faculties,—the Feelings, or capacities of Pleasure and Pain,—and the Exertive or Conative Powers, —I do not propose as original. It was first promulgated by Kant (footnote by the Ed. "Kritik der Urtheilskraft," Einleitung. The same division is also adopted as the basis of his "Anthropologie"); and the felicity of the distribution was so apparent, that it has now been all but universally adopted in Germany by the philosophers of every school. . . To the psychologists of this country, it is apparently unknown. They still adhere to the old scholastic division into powers of the Understanding and powers of the Will; or, as it is otherwise expressed, into Intellectual and Active Powers." Hamilton, "Metaphysics," p. 129.
58. Jones, pp. 49-54.
59. E.g., "Notes on Mind," Dwight, Vol. I, p. 693, Note 70 *et passim.*
60. *Ibid.*, p. 669 *et passim.* Note 34 is a remarkable statement of Idealism. His statements about the Association of Ideas (Notes on Mind) are close to Hume's position, in fact, Jones says (p. 53) that Edwards' doctrine "so far as it is developed is equal to Hume's doctrine."
61. "In consequence of an earlier revival in his parish of Northampton, his attention had been drawn to the little-understood psychology of the awakening soul, and with the detachment of the scientist he set himself to study the problem. The terrors aroused by his minatory sermons provided his clinical laboratory with numberous cases of abnormal emotionalism. Day after day he probed and analyzed and compared . . . like a modern psychologist he was at enormous pains to chart the successive steps in the miraculous transformation." Parrington, I, p. 160. See also Allen, pp. 133-160; Edwards, "Narrative of Surprising Conversations," "Treatise on the Religious Affections," etc.

62. Thomas Clap, 1703-1767. Born at Scituate, Mass., about three months before Jonathan Edwards. Entered Harvard at the age of 15, and was graduated in 1722. Pastor at Windham until 1739. The following year he followed Elisha Williams as Rector of Yale, where he stimulated the study of science, drew up a new Code of Laws, made improvements in the library, and added to the college buildings. Vigorous and assertive, he became unpopular, and resigned in 1765, "in consequence of his age and infirmities, and strong desire of private life." He lived but a short time in his retirement, and died the following year at the age of 64. His writings include an "Introduction to the Study of Philosophy," 1743, and an "Essay on the Nature and Foundation of Moral Virtue and Obligation," 1765. In his Literary Diary (quoted in Sprague) Stiles gives a vivid picture of President Clap, his learning and his "happy and advantageous method of reading." Park paints a different picture ("J. Edwards, The Fiery Puritan," p. 110).

Sprague, "Annals of the American Pulpit"; "Dictionary of American Biography." Discussed by Jones, pp. 18-21, and Townsend, p. 25.

63. A rare book. Copies at Yale and at Union Theological Seminary. Clap cites or refers to Norris, "Ideal World" (of which he professes to follow the sentiments and expressions), Cotton Mather, Wollebius, Campbell, Gastrell, Cumberland, Hutcheson, Locke, S. Clarke, Wollaston (whom Stiles gives as the source of Clap's Moral Philosophy), Grove, Jenkins, Williots, Leland, Patten, Taylor, Pool, van Maastricht, Grotius, Puffendorf, Ames, Socrates, Plato, several Church Fathers, and the Bible, all in a book of 66 pages.

64. Self-Interest (Campbell), pp. 13 ff.; Universal Benevolence (Cumberland), pp. 17 ff.; Moral Sense (Hutcheson), pp. 22 ff.; Reason, pp. 25 ff.; Moral Fitness of Things (Clarke), pp. 30 ff.; Conformity to Truth (Wollaston), pp. 33 ff.; Intuitive Ideas of Right and Wrong, pp. 35 ff.; Obedience to the Will and Commands of God with a view to obtaining Favor and promoting individual Happiness, pp. 38 ff.; and

Eclective Systems (Grove), mixing various of these standards, p. 40.

65. Riley, "American Thought," pp. 26-28.

66. Schneider, II, p. 328.

67. Allen, p. 299.

CHAPTER TWO

1. McCosh, J., "The Scottish Philosophy," N. Y., Carter, 1874, 481 pp., pp. 2-10 (condensed).

2. Morais, H. M., "Deism in 18th Century America," N. Y., Col. Univ. Press, 1934, 203 pp., p. 120.

3. Adams, J. T., "History of the United States," II, p. 208.

4. Cubberley, E. P., "Public Education in the U. S.," Boston, Houghton Mifflin, 1934, Rev. Ed., 782 pp., p. 82.

5. Beard, C. A. and M. R., "The Rise of American Civilization," N. Y., Macmillan, 1933, 824, 865 pp., I, p. 815.

6. Cubberley, *op. cit.*, p. 249.

7. Schmidt, G. P., "The Old Time College President," N. Y., Col. Univ. Press, 1930, 251 pp., pp. 39-41. Snow, L. F., "The College Curriculum in the U. S.," N. Y., Teachers College, Col. Univ., 1907, 186 pp., pp. 141 ff.

8. Published 1828, Vol. XV of the *American Journal of Science;* see Snow, *op. cit.*, pp. 145-154, for a summary.

9. Snow, pp. 140-141, Schmidt, *op. cit.*, has an excellent chapter entitled The Bearer of the Old Tradition, pp. 108-145, which describes minutely the content of the old undifferentiated course in Moral Philosophy.

10. Snow, *passim.*

11. Foster, *op. cit.*, p. 243.

12. 1738-1812. Born in the Bavarian Palatinate. Educated at Marburg and Heidelberg. Landed at Philadelphia in 1764, preached in Pennsylvania and New York until 1784, when in the organization of King's College as Columbia he became Professor of German and Geography, continuing meanwhile to preach in New York and vicinity. Became Professor of Moral Philosophy in 1789, and resigned in 1795. "His course in this department was a marvel of thorough-

ness." Mathews, B., *et al.*, editors, "A History of Columbia University," 1754-1904, N. Y., Col. Univ. Press, 1904, 493 pp., pp. 64, 69-73, 80. Obituary in N. Y. *Columbian*, June 5, 1812. "Dictionary of Am. Biog." Discussed by Schmidt, Ch. IV, *passim*.

13. From the title page of the "Natural Principles of Rectitude."

14. New York, printed by T. and J. Swords, Printers to the Faculty of Physics of Columbia College, 1795. Copy at Columbia. Sources: The author "has consulted, but not in a servile manner followed authors of fame and great authority—he has even taken the liberty to differ from them in many points of no small importance" (p. ix). The only definite authorities cited are Paley, Hutcheson, Blackstone, and Vatel. Gros probably followed the scholastic tradition in psychology as handed down by the German theologians with whom he was familiar.

15. Chapter I, Of the actions of man, and their morality or immorality. The rest of the section is an analysis of Gros' psychology, documented by citations from pages 11-19.

16. See Maher, "Psychology," pp. 28-41.

17. Maher's "Psychology," revised in 1900, reprinted in 1933 from the Ninth Edition of 1918, is an elaboration in modern terms of the positions taken by Gros in 1795 (both resting on Aquinas' formulations of Aristotle).

18. Schmidt, p. 142.

19. 1722-1794. Born in Scotland. Studied for seven years at the University of Edinburgh, being graduated at the age of 21. Preached in Scotland until called in 1768 to be President of the College of New Jersey, where he remained until his death. As Sprague says: "He introduced at once, many important improvements in the system of education, and gave to the institution a more vigorous intellectual tone, and greatly improved its reputation abroad." He taught composition, taste and criticism, chronology and history, moral philosophy, and divinity. James Madison was one of his pupils, and testified to the value of the course in Moral Philosophy ("Life and Times of Madison," by W. C. Rives, quoted by McCosh, "Scottish Philosophy," p. 187). He was a mem-

ber of the Continental Congress, a signer of the Constitu-
tion, and an ardent patriot. Life in Sprague, "Annals of the
Am. Pulpit," with extensive quotations from a "Memoir" by
Ashbel Green, a later President of Princeton. Discussed by
McCosh, "Scottish Phil.," pp. 184-190; Riley, "Am.
Thought," pp. 125-133; Riley, "Am. Phil.," pp. 483-496;
Townsend, pp. 73-74, 103; and Tyler, M. C., "The Lit-
erary History of the American Revolution," N. Y., Putnam,
1897, 2 vols., 521, 527 pp., Vol. II, pp. 319-330.

20. Riley, *op. cit.*, p. 129.

21. Schmidt, p. 122. See also Miller, S., "Brief Retrospect of the
18th Century," N. Y., Swords, 1803, 2 vols., 544, 510 pp.,
Vol. II, p. 377.

22. Vol. I, pp. 267-374. Reprinted, edited by V. L. Collins,
Princeton Univ. Press, 1912.

23. Editor's Preface, "Witherspoon's Works," Edition of 1800.
Sources: He cites or refers to Hobbes, Locke, Reid, Hutcheson, Clarke, Wollaston, Campbell, A. Smith, Hume, Butler,
Wilson, Ricalton, Baxter, Mandeville, Collins, Nettleton,
Kames, Balfour, Beattie, Leibniz, Jonathan Edwards. In the
recapitulation he adds references to Balguy, Leland, and
writers on government and politics.

24. A term employed by Thomas Reid, and subjected to a searching historical critique by Hamilton, "Reid's Works," Note A,
pp. 742-803.

25. Principally Hutcheson, Reid, and Beattie. See McCosh, "Scottish Philosophy," and Laurie, H., "Scottish Philosophy,"
Glasgow, Maclehose, 1902, 344 pp.

26. P. 275. This threefold division gave way immediately to
Reid's division into the Understanding and the Active
Powers.

27. Passions, pp. 276-8; Taste, as the Scotch school called it, pp.
280-5.

28. P. 279. Witherspoon found Berkeleyanism at the College when
he came, especially in the persons of Mr. Periam and Stanhope Smith. He ridiculed it, argued it down, gave his daugh-
ter in marriage to Smith, who formally renounced his here-
sies, and fell in line for the Presidency. The story is told

by Ashbel Green and quoted with glee by McCosh, p. 188. See also Riley, "Am. Thought," pp. 127 ff.; Beasley, "Search for Truth," p. ii.

29. 1750-1819. Born in Lancaster County, Penn. Prepared in his father's Academy, he was sent to Princeton in his 16th year, and entered the Junior Class. After graduation he taught for a time in his father's school, went back to Princeton for two years as Tutor, became a missionary in West Virginia, and helped establish Hampden Sidney College, of which he became President. In 1799 he returned to Princeton again, this time as Professor of Moral Philosophy, and became President in 1794, having for some years discharged the duties of the office during the absence and later the blindness of John Witherspoon. Long in poor health, he resigned in 1812.

His writings include an "Essay on the Causes of the Variety of Complexion and Figure of the Human Species," 1797, and the Lectures cited in the text. Sprague, "Annals of the Am. Pulpit." Discussed by McCosh, p. 188; Riley, "Am. Thought," pp. 130-133; Riley, "Am. Phil.," pp. 497-508; Schmidt, pp. 114 ff.

30. Sprague, III, p. 336.

31. Trenton, Fenton, 1812, Vol. I, 14 Lectures in 324 pages. Vol. II is devoted to Natural Theology, Oeconomics, and Political Philosophy. Sources: Smith cites or refers to Hobbes, Locke, Berkeley, Hume, Porter, Monboddo, Priestley, Reid, Hartley, Hutcheson, Beattie, Ferguson, Stewart, Campbell, Watts, Kames, Clarke, Shaftesbury, Paley, Derham, Ray, Doddridge; Descartes, Volney, Montesquieu, Helvetius, Malebranche, Bonnet; Leibniz; J. Edwards, Witherspoon; and Pythagoras, Aristotle, Cicero, Lucretius, and Plutarch.

32. Pp. 300-310. See the whole lecture, pp. 300-324, which includes a critique of Paley.

33. Schmidt, p. 108.

34. 1766-1844. Born at Warwick, Mass. Graduated from Harvard in 1792. From 1795 to 1800 he was a tutor, annually appointed, but in 1800 became the first "permanent tutor." In 1810 he became Professor of Logic and Metaphysics, and

in 1827, Alford Professor of Natural Religion, Moral Philosophy and Civil Polity, remaining in this position until 1827. Besides the Logic, he edited an edition of Brown's "Lectures on the Philosophy of the Human Mind," 1827. "Dictionary of Am. Biog." See also Quincy, "History of Harvard," *passim;* Rand, "Philosophical Instruction in Harvard University from 1636 to 1906," *Harvard Grads. Mag.,* Sept., 1928, pp. 42-43. Discussed by Townsend, pp. 100-101.

35. The edition of 1849, printed on entirely new plates, but with no alteration from previous editions, contains 178 pages, of which pages 13-30 contain the psychology. The Logic is based on "An Essay on the Elements, Principles, and different Modes of Reasoning," by Richard Kirwan, with references to Collard, Watts ("Logic," and "Improvement of the Mind"), Tatham's "Chart and Scale of Truth," Gambier's "Introduction to Moral Evidence," Condillac, Gilbert, Demoivre, Aristotle (with Reid's Analysis), and Bacon. Other sources cited in the Preface, footnotes, and Concluding Remarks are: Locke, Reid, Stewart, Beattie, Campbell, Belsham, Scott, Burgersdicius, Le Clerc, Duncan, Buffier, Berkeley, Hume, Wollaston, Baxter, Hume, etc. The reference to Brown on page 170 must have been added at a later date than the first edition (Brown's Lectures, 1820). The book received a 15-page review in the *North American Review,* Nov., 1816, pp. 78-92, with an interesting résumé of the history of Logic and logic teaching in the universities, and a keen critique of Stewart.

36. 1745-1813. Born near Philadelphia. Graduated at the College of New Jersey in 1760, studied medicine with Dr. John Redman in Philadelphia until 1766, when he went to Edinburgh to continue his studies, spending two years there, and finishing in London and Paris. In 1769 he became Professor of Chemistry at the College of Philadelphia, and in 1789, Professor of the Theory and Practice of Medicine. In 1791 the College became the University of Pennsylvania, and Rush took over three departments, Institutes and Practice of Medicine, Clinical Practice, and (in 1796) Practice of Physic, remaining active in these departments until his death.

He was an ardent patriot, and a signer of the Declaration of Independence. He was a founder of Dickinson College (see Goodman, 321-41). At the time of his death he was Treasurer of the U. S. Mint. Zimmerman writes: "Sa conduite a merité que non seulement la ville de Philadelphie, mais l'Humanité entière lui élève une statue," referring to Rush's services during the fever of 1793 (quoted by Allibone), and a tribute in the *North American Review* of Oct., 1860, closes by calling him "applauded by angels and numbered with the just." Allibone, "Dictionary of Authors"; Chalmer's "Biographical Dictionary." Discussed by Riley, "Am. Thought," pp. 104-117 *et passim*. See also Goodman, N. G., "Benjamin Rush, Physician and Citizen," Philadelphia, U. of Penn. Press, 1934, 421 pp., especially pp. 255-271, 274 ff., 278 ff., 292-295, 307-320, and Sigerist, H. E., "American Medicine," N. Y., Norton, 1934, 316 pp., pp. 81-87.

37. Goodman, p. 352.
38. Dr. Thomas Young in the 7th Ed. of the Encyclopaedia Britannica.
39. Allibone, Article "Benjamin Rush."
40. "American Thought," p. 105.
41. On the influence of physical causes, in promoting the strength and activity of the intellectual faculties of man, pp. 88-119. Lecture 11 discusses the utility to a physician of a knowledge of the faculties and operations of the human mind. Two additional lectures are given on the pleasures of the senses and of the mind, with an inquiry into their proximate cause.
42. Ch. 3, An Inquiry into the Influence of Physical Causes upon the Moral Faculty; Ch. 4, An Account of the Influence of the Military and Political Events of the American Revolution upon the Human Body; Ch. 5, An Inquiry into the Relation of Tastes and Aliments to each other, and into the influence of this relation upon Health and Pleasure; Ch. 7, An Inquiry into the Effects of Ardent Spirits upon the Human Body and Mind; Ch. 14, An Account of the state of the Body and Mind in Old Age.

43. "Medical Inquiries and Observations upon the Diseases of the Mind," 1st Ed., 1812, 367 pp.

44. "Diseases of the Mind," p. 10.

45. See Goodman, pp. 292-95.

46. Introductory Lectures, p. 271.

47. *Ibid.*, p. 256.

48. Goodman, p. 345. See "Diseases of the Mind," pp. 105 ff., 204 ff., 274 (technique of re-education), *et passim*. See also Riley, "Am. Thought," 110.

49. Goodman, p. 265.

50. Riley, *op. cit.*, p. 109. Rush, "Different Species of Phobia and Mania."

51. "Diseases of the Mind," pp. 303-4.

52. *Inter alios*, Abercrombie, Beasley, and Upham.

53. 1777-1845. Born near Edenton, N. C. Graduated from the College of New Jersey in 1797. Became tutor and studied under Stanhope Smith from 1797 to 1799. Rector of the Episcopal Churches at Elizabethtown, Albany, and Baltimore in turn until 1813, when he became Provost of the Univ. of Penn., and Professor of Moral Philosophy. Resigned in 1828, became Rector at Trenton, then retired to Elizabethtown. "Dictionary of Am. Biog;" Sprague's "Annals of the Am. Pulpit"; Discussed by Riley, "American Phil.," Book V, Ch. 7, pp. 519-536, and "Am. Thought," pp. 112, 135-6; Blakey, IV, pp. 520-522.

54. From the Dedication to Bishop Hobart. He writes further: "You are aware that in the College of Princeton, to which we were attached, after the fanciful theory of Bishop Berkeley, as a kind of philosophical daydream, had maintained its prevalence for a season; the principles of Reid and the Scottish metaphysicians superseded it, and during the period of our residence in the seminary, acquired and maintained undisputed sway. At that time, I, together with all those graduates who took any interest in the subject, embraced without doubt or hesitation the doctrines of the Scottish school" (p. ii).

55. Philadelphia, Potter, 1822. Part Second was never published.

56. P. 117, "A ranker and more poisonous weed of atheism never

sprang from the teeming garden of Epicurus, than that which has been planted and brought to maturity, and distributed among mankind in various infusions, by the great modern sceptick of Scotland." P. 85, "Mr. Hume's principles reconcilable to theism! Placidis coeant immitia, serpentes avibus geninentur, tigribus agni." *Ibid.*

57. Schmidt, p. 123, footnote. See also Riley, "Am. Phil.," Book V, Ch. 6.

58. Riley, "Am. Thought," p. 121.

59. Vol. II, p. 10.

60. 1752-1836. Born at Stonington, Conn. Graduated from Dartmouth in 1777 ("he was one of those engaged in cutting away the forest trees from the spot on which the College edifices now stand"). From 1779 until his death he was pastor of the Congregational Church in the little town of Thetford, Vt., where in addition to his pastoral duties he prepared between 1786 and 1816 some 60 young men for the ministry. "He was a man of uncommon intellectual powers. . . Though his library was small, and his reading by no means extensive, he was familiar with the ablest writers on metaphysical science. . . He used to say that he had spent more than three months of intense study upon three words,—free-moral-agency. Nor was the time spent in vain; for he acquired a knowledge of the mind, and its operations, which comparatively few have ever reached." (Letter of David Thurston in Sprague's "Annals"). "Dictionary of Am. Biog.;" Sprague's "Annals of the Am. Pulpit." Discussed by Foster, "Genetic History of New England Theology," pp. 242-245; Blakey, IV, pp. 522-523.

61. West, Samuel, "Essays on Liberty and Necessity," New Bedford, Spooner, 1793; re-issued in 1795 with a second part, 96 pp., p. 12. Answered by Jonathan Edwards, Junior, "Dissertation concerning Liberty and Necessity," Works, Vol. I, pp. 295-468. See also Foster, pp. 232-242.

62. "Works," 4 Vols. "Moral Government," Vols. II and III in "Works." See also Foster, pp. 246-249; Fisher, G. P., "Discussions in History and Theology," N. Y., Scribner, 1880, 555 pp., pp. 285-354.

63. Portland, Printed at the Mirror Office, 1824, 414 pp., of which the first 94 contain the essentials of Burton's psychology. Sources: No citations or quotations except from the Bible. One reference to Locke. The work is based on "reason and scripture" (p. 20). See chronological table in the Appendix for authors he might have read. His book was published in 1824, but "the work was written some twenty years before it was published; but it was finally printed with scarcely any variations from the original manuscript" (Sprague). Burton gives no hint of knowing Tetens or Kant.

64. Ely, "Conversations," Philadelphia, Printed for the Author, 1819, 228 pp., small size; p. 20. "The sources whence he has drawn his doctrines, are his own consciousness, memory, and reflection; and the writings of Locke, Hume, Price, Hartley, Lord Kames, Reid, Stewart, Duncan, President Edwards, Beattie, Watts, Condillac, and Cogan. . . He disclaims all metaphysics but those of common sense" (Preface). He coins a new term, "Anthropsychia, the science of the human soul, which is rather indefinitely called 'The Philosophy of the Human Mind' " (p. 13). Note the Chapter on Comparative Mental Science, pp. 208-217.

65. Bain, "Senses and the Intellect," 1855; Spencer, "Psychology," 1855; Sully, "Outlines" (the first British book comparable to Upham's), 1884. An extended review of Upham in the *British Quarterly Review* of Feb., 1847, laments the fact that there was no similar book in England at the time.

66. Review of Upham, Schmucker and Tappan, *British Quarterly Review*, Feb., 1847, pp. 88-119. This citation from pp. 92-93.

67. Foster, *op. cit.*, p. 249.

68. "A more or less complete oblivion has now fallen upon such names as that of the Rev. H. P. Tappan, Professor of Intellectual and Moral Philosophy in New York, who attacked the work of Edwards in 1839; or that of Thomas C. Upham, whose "Elements of Mental Philosophy" persisted from 1831 to 1848, and still lingers on the book-shelves of literary antiquarians." Brett, III, 256. Mr. Brett apparently

did not know that Tappan became Chancellor of the University of Michigan, our first real University in the European sense. Upham's books were still reprinted and sold in 1886-7. This is a fair sample of Brett's inadequate, inaccurate, and unbalanced treatment of early American psychology.

69. "An innovation of a different kind was made in 1844 [Brett is wrong again, the work was copyrighted and issued in 1842] by S. S. Schmucker in a work entitled 'Psychology or Elements of a New System of Mental Philosophy.' This work was based on conceptions more allied to the philosophy of Leibniz than to that of Reid; it received favourable notice from Beneke in his review of the state of psychology at that time, but neither Schmucker nor his work appears to have exerted any extensive influence." Brett, III, 256-7. Brett is guessing. The reviewer on the *British Quarterly Review* demonstrates by a careful analysis of Schmucker's work that in spite of its curious terminology "his doctrines are not fundamentally distinct from those of recent writers of the Anglo-Scottish school" (p. 104); see also p. 102, *et passim*.

70. Mahan, "Intellectual Philosophy," 1st Ed., 1845, pp. iii-iv.

71. "Among those who showed distinctly the influence of Kant was Laurens P. Hickok, author of a 'Rational Psychology' (1848) and an 'Empirical Psychology' (1854)." Brett, III, p. 257.

72. Hickok, "Rational Psychology," 1848, p. 18.

73. 1799-1872. Born at Deerfield, N. H. Graduated from Dartmouth in 1818, and from Andover Theological Seminary in 1821, remaining at the latter institution for a year as Assistant Professor of Hebrew. Pastor of the Congregational Church of Rochester, N. H., until 1824, when he became Professor of Mental and Moral Philosophy at Bowdoin College. He was active in this department until 1867, when he became Professor Emeritus. Allibone cites fifteen works from his pen. Appleton's "Cyc. of Am. Biog."; Allibone, "Dictionary of Authors." Discussed by Blakey, IV, 523-530 (the whole discussion obviously based on the review in the

British Quarterly Review, cited above); Brett, III, p. 256.

74. Portland, 1827, 576 pp. A rare book. Copy of the 2nd Ed., 1828, at Union Theological Seminary.

75. Boston and Portland, 1831.

76. Intellectual philosophy obviously excluded any consideration of the sensibilities and the will. See Porter, "The Human Intellect," p. 5.

"Man is not a simple, but a combined or complex existence, made up of *intellect* and matter. It belongs to *Intellectual* Philosophy to make inquiries into his *intellectual* part, into that characteristic element in his formation, which thinks, feels, wills, and combines." "Int. Phil.," p. 13. The 1832 abridgment, entitled "Mental Philosophy," simply changes intellect to *mind,* and intellectual to *mental,* otherwise retaining the definition.

77. "Mental Philosophy," 1st Ed., Ch. 13, pp. 188-197.

78. *Ibid.,* p. 196.

79. Portland, 1834, 399 pp.; later incorporated into the two-volume work as an integral part of the system.

80. "Treatise on the Will," 1st Ed., p. 20.

81. See *ante,* p. 81, for the complete citation.

82. "Mental Philosophy," 1869 Ed., Vol. I, pp. 51-61. (This and all following quotations will be made from the definitive edition of 1869.) He appeals to the evidence of consciousness, the testimony of language, incidental remarks by various writers, and especially by writers on the philosophy of mind, including Locke, Hume, Kames, Mackintosh, Burton, and Théry. A quotation from Shakespeare is particularly pat:

"It shows a will most incorrect to heaven,
A heart unfortified—
An understanding simple and unschool'd."
—HAMLET, Act. I, Scene 2.

He sums up thus: "For the reasons which have been given, we find ourselves authorized . . . in arranging the states, exercises, or acts of the mind . . . under the *three* general heads of Intellectual, Sentimentive or Sentient, and Volitional" (p. 60).

83. See Upham, I, pp. 92-94, 254-255.
84. *British Quarterly Review, loc. cit.*, pp. 110-111.
85. *Ibid.*, pp. 98, 116.
86. The 1827 book is decidedly Lockian in spirit and terminology. He cites or refers to Bacon, Locke, Cudworth, Berkeley, Hume, Hartley; Hutcheson, Reid, Beattie, Oswald, Stewart, Brown, Priestley; More, Wollaston, Butler, Price, Clarke, King, Chubb; Duncan, Watts, Gambier, A. Smith, Mackintosh; Campbell, Harris, Tooke; Hogarth, Reynolds, Alison, Burke, J. G. Cooper, Cogan; Edwards; Feinagle; Barrow, Jenyn, Good; Montaigne, Descartes, Malebranche, Buffier, Condillac, de Tracy, Diderot, Helvétius, Cabanis, Buffon, de Staël; Pinel, Esquirol, Hibbert, Rush (abnormal psychology); Brucker, de Gérando, Bayle, New Edinburgh Encyclopaedia, Dictionaire des Sciences Médicales; Kant; Aristotle, Cicero, Longinus.

In the 1840 edition in two volumes his heaviest direct borrowings are from Reid (375 lines), Stewart (175), Brown (84), Locke (165), Cudworth (98), and Buffon (one citation of 145 lines). However, large amounts are taken indirectly from Reid and Stewart, perhaps by unconscious plagiarism, perhaps because the sources were so familiar to the reader as not to need reference. E.g., Vol. I, pp. 175-179, are almost verbally taken from Stewart's "Elements" without a word of acknowledgment.

87. "Primary truths, Upham, after Stewart, defines, as 'Such, and such only, as can neither be proved nor refuted by other propositions of greater perspicuity.' Under the names of first truths, first principles, common sense, intuitive truths and principles; similar views have been advanced by Buffier, Beattie, Reid, Campbell, Brown, and others." *British Quarterly Review*, p. 99. Upham names six: Original and authoritative *grounds of belief*; reality and certainty of our *personal existence*; belief and certainty of our *personal identity*; existence of the external, *material world*; confidence in the *memory*; and confidence in human *testimony*. Ch. II, "Intellectual Philosophy." (This list varies somewhat in later editions.)

88. In 1831, in addition to the French writers cited above in the 1827 work, he refers to Théry, Sicard, Cousin, Gassendi, Condorcet, Jouffroy, d'Alembert, and Voltaire.

89. "Continental influences were at work in the decade of 1830 to 1840, and one of the most widely circulated books of that period was Henry's translation of Cousin's 'Lectures on Locke' (New York, 1834)." Brett, III, p. 257.

90. His first published work was a translation of Jahn's "Biblical Archaeology," characterized as a "faithful translation" (Allibone). He cites Kant without translation.

91. Blakey remarks three times on Upham's lack of originality (but note the careful analyses of Vaughn), although admitting that "there is a healthy spirit of philosophical discussion pervading the whole" (IV, p. 530). Brett says: "Originality is the feature most conspicuous by its absence throughout this literary tradition. . . Upham was infinitesimally original and shone by comparison; he wrote a separate treatise on 'Imperfect and Disordered Mental Action' (1840), which pointed to a less stereotyped activity than that of his contemporaries" (III, p. 256). Brett is strangely unfair in his whole treatment of early American psychology, and neither he nor Blakey realized the originality of Upham in developing without precedent a new and effective presentation of (largely, but not wholly) old material. In the works of 1827, 1831 and later editions, Upham experimented in varying the order of topics. A study of the tables of contents of these editions presents a vivid picture of an orderly mind working over his material and getting it finally into the best possible arrangement.

92. "The general classification is clear, natural, and comprehensive. The subordinate divisions are also natural and explicit, so that the mind passes, by a kind of natural succession, from one topic to another. Nor is the essential unity of the mind ever lost sight of." 1839, Critique of Upham's work by D. W. Clark, A.M., Principal of the Amenia (N. Y.) Seminary.

93. "Int. Phil.," 1827, 1928; "Mental Phil.," 2 vols., 1831, 1833, 1837, 1839, 1840, 1843, 1848, 1869 (including the will);

Abridgment, 1832 (3rd Ed.), 1840, 1848, 1851, 1861, and many times reprinted up to (at least) 1881. Perhaps other editions also that have not come to my attention.

94. "It is now used, I believe, in most of our literary institutions." 1839, Letter of S. Luckey, D.D., Editor of the *Christian Advocate and Journal, Quarterly Review*, etc. Used for at least one year (1840) by Professor Walker at Harvard. See Rand, article cited in *Harvard Grads. Mag.*, pp. 188-200.

95. Vol. I, Part Third, Imperfect and Disordered Intellectual Action, pp. 453-500. Vol. II, Part Third, Imperfect or Disordered Sentimentive Action, pp. 403-455. Disorders of the Will are taken up in Division Three, Part Three, Freedom of the Will, Ch. VII, Enthralment or Slavery of the Will, Vol. II, pp. 617-631.

96. Outlines of Imperfect and Disordered Mental Action, 1840, 399 pp. Certainly not as original as the pioneer work of Rush, but still entitled to rank as the first systematic text on the subject. The treatise follows the development of the main work point by point, and discusses under each head what the author calls "imperfect or disordered action."

97. "Mental Philosophy," 1st Ed., p. 4.

98. *British Quarterly Review, loc. cit.*, pp. 108, 109-110.

99. "In the . . . chapters . . . devoted to an explication of the phenomena of the different senses . . . the explications of sensation . . . are, for the most part, similar to the views maintained by the Anglo-Scottish writers. . .

"Closely connected with this subject, is that of Perception. Upham's notions on this point show a strong bias towards the sentiments of Reid and his disciples. . . *His exposition is, perhaps, on the whole, more consistent and more scientifically stated than Reid's.*" *British Quarterly Review*, p. 102. (Italics mine.)

100. "The intellectual states of the mind . . . I consider as all referable to two generic susceptibilities,—those of Simple Suggestion and Relative Suggestion." Thomas Brown, "Lectures on the Philosophy of the Human Mind," Lecture 33. See Lectures 33-34, for Simple Suggestion; 45-51 for Relative Suggestion. For Upham's treatment, see I, pp. 255-281.

101. *British Quarterly Review*, pp. 104, 117.

102. *Ibid.*, pp. 104, 105, 106, 117.

103. "The name pathematic, which Upham applies to the sensibilities of the first part of this division, he has avowedly borrowed from Sir James (Mackintosh)." *British Quarterly Review*, p. 105. See Mackintosh, "Dissertation on the Progress of Ethical Philosophy," 3rd Edition, p. 203 (article on Hartley).

104. *Op. cit.*, pp. 251-252.

105. See Vol. I, pp. 47, 65-82; Vol. II, pp. 62, 273, *et passim*.

106. I, pp. 69-70; II, p. 101, *et passim*.

107. II, pp. 62-63, 283, 352-4, 356.

108. *Op. cit.*, p. 149.

109. *Op. cit.*, p. 20.

110. *British Quarterly Review*, p. 118.

111. "The Mental Guide, being a Compend of the First Principles of Metaphysics, and a System of attaining an easy and correct mode of Thought and Style by Transcription, predicated on the Analysis of the Human Mind. For Schools and Academies," Anonymous, Boston, 1828, 384 pp., dedicated to Levi Hedge. Pp. 13-72 contain the psychology, an exact transcription of portions of Locke's "Essay" and a few borrowings from Reid and Stewart without quotation marks or indications of the source other than the statement in the Preface. A rather good selection and arrangement of topics. Pp. 73-88, entitled Consequentiae, make a practical application to literary composition, and the rest of the book consists of well-chosen literary selections for study and paraphrase in the words of the student.

112. "The Elements of Moral Science," Boston, 1835; the edition printed in 1847 is marked 31st thousand, 396 pp. The popularity and sale of this book was astonishing. It represents Wayland's revolt against Paley, whose works were the standard texts when W. began teaching Moral Philosophy in Brown. He admits the greatest obligations to Bishop Butler, especially in the doctrine of the Conscience. See Preface.

113. "Phrenology, Proved, Illustrated and Applied," O. S. and

L. N. Fowler, assisted by Samuel Kirkham, N. Y., 1836, running into the 13th edition by 1842, 430 pp. The quotation is from the Preface. See also Brett, III, pp. 28, 257, *et passim*; Boring, pp. 47-57; Flugel, pp. 36-45; Branch, E. D., "The Sentimental Years," N. Y., Appleton, 1935, 432 pp., pp. 278-288; Boehme, M. P., "Phrenology, An Early Attempt to Find an Index of Intelligence," unpublished Master's Thesis, 1933, Rutgers Univ.

114. 1788-1865. Elizabeth Stryker, born in New Utrecht, L. I. Educated by private tutors. Married Dr. J. B. Ricord in 1810. In 1829 she opened a young ladies' seminary in Geneva, N. Y., of which she was Principal until 1842. Appleton's "Cyc. of Am. Biog."

115. Geneva, 1839, 408 pp. Sources: Hume, Stewart, Coleridge; Cousin, Descartes, Montaigne, Rousseau, Jouffroy; Mason, Upham, Combe, Leibniz; Paley and Brougham are cited or referred to, but the work is "based on the Truth as we find it revealed in the Sacred Scriptures, and is not intended to enter into the intricate disquisitions of the Metaphysical Schools" (Preface).

Part First discusses the existence and immateriality of the soul. Part Second treats of Consciousness, Sensation, Attention, Conception, Memory, Association, Abstraction, Reason and Understanding, Judgment, and Imagination, after making the point that "the soul or mind has no parts, it knows, feels, wills and reasons; and these faculties are all concerned in its operations, perhaps constitute all that we can at present know of the soul" (p. 60). Part Third deals with Feeling, Taste, and the Emotions; and Part Fourth with the Moral Sense, Conscience and Moral Responsibility.

116. 1807-1898. Born at Pinckney, N. Y. Graduated from Hamilton College in 1828. Studied theology at Princeton for two years, and became a Presbyterian minister. President of Central College, Ohio, 1842-7. Appleton, "Cyc. of Am. Biog."

117. New Haven, 1839, 316 pp. He divides the phenomena of the mind which are the objects of consciousness into

Sensation, Ideas, Emotions, Affections, Desires, and Acts of Will (pp. 19, 20). In a concluding chapter on the Origin and Derivation of Mind, he asserts that "the ultimate origin of all finite minds is by immediate creation" (p. 307). The author hints at a familiarity with Locke, Stewart, Brown, Kant, Cousin, and others, as well as ancient writers, but makes no specific references. I find him quoted by only one later American writer, Winslow, who quotes nearly everybody. *Vide infra.*

118. Blakey, IV, p. 542.

119. 1805-1881. Born in Rhinebeck, N. Y. Graduated from Union College in 1825, and from Auburn Theological Seminary in 1827. After a brief service in the ministry he became Professor of Moral Philosophy in the University of the City of New York, 1832-38. In 1852 he was elected the first Chancellor of the University of Michigan. Retired in 1863, and spent the rest of his life in Europe. Appleton, "Cyc. of Am. Biog."

120. See Cubberley, "Public Education in the U. S.," pp. 274, 275, 278, 340.

121. "A Review of Edwards' Inquiry into the Freedom of the Will, containing I. Statement of Edwards' System. II. The Legitimate Consequences of this System. III. An Examination of the Arguments against a Self-Determining Will," New York, 1839, 300 pp.

122. N. Y., 1840, 318 pp.

123. "The Doctrine of the Will, applied to Moral Agency and Responsibility," N. Y., 1841, 348 pp.

124. "Elements of Logic," N. Y., 1844; 1855 ed., 467 pp.

125. *British Quarterly Review, loc. cit.,* p. 118.

126. Montpelier, 1820, 215 pp.

127. New Haven, 1838, 200 pp.

128. New Haven, 1841, 340 pp.

129. "Examination of Edwards," pp. 11-12.

130. "Power of the Will," p. 40.

131. 1806-1841. Born in Kirschbracht, Prussia. Studied at Marburg, Giessen and Heidelberg (under Karl Daub). Came to America as a political refugee, and after some minor

teaching experience became organizer and first President of Marshall College in 1836. "Dictionary of Am. Biog."

132. "Psychology, or, a View of the Human Soul; including Anthropology," N. Y., 1840; 2nd Ed., revised and improved, 1841, 401 pp. "The present work is, as far as the author knows, the first attempt to unite German and American mental philosophy" (p. v). Sources: "The author feels himself under obligation to acknowledge fully the use he has made of the following authors: Locke, D. Stewart, Reid, Brown, Rosenkranz, Carus, Jr., Carus, Ser., Daub, Stiedenroth, Suabedissen, Eschenmeyer, Heinroth, Hegel, Kant, Wirth, Steffens, Herbart, Hartman, and others. He has used these authorities with more or less freedom, and especially Carus, Jr., Daub, and Rosenkranz" (p. vi). In addition I find references to Whately, Kames, Schubert, and Gall.

Blakey (IV, p. 541) characterizes it as "a very excellent and common-sense publication, and has been well-received in the United States." Discussed by Townsend, pp. 81-82. Orestes A. Brownson hailed it as a work of genius. "Dict. of Am. Biog." See also Murdock, J., "Sketches of Modern Philosophy," Hartford, Wells, 1842, 201 pp., pp. 189-201. (A rare book, but liberally cited in the Appendix to Townsend.)

133. Hamilton, "Lectures on Metaphysics," Lecture VIII.

134. Rauch, p. 185. "As a transcendental philosopher, Dr. Rauch belonged to the school of Hegel. . . If I have not entirely misunderstood him, he is a Transcendentalist and a Pantheist of the school of Hegel." Murdock, *op. cit.*, pp. 194, 199. Rauch's thesis anticipates the position of Strong, C. A., "Why the Mind Has a Body," N. Y., Macmillan, 1903, 355 pp.

135. 1799-1873. Born Hagerstown, Md. Graduated from Princeton in 1820. Pastor at Frederick, Md., until 1826, when he became Chairman of the faculty of the Theological Seminary at Gettysburg, Pa., and for four years the only instructor. His various published works number more than a hundred. Appleton, "Cyc. of Am. Biog."

136. N. Y., 1842; 2nd Ed., much enlarged, 1855, 329 pp. Re-

viewed by Blakey, IV, 530-534, and in the article already
cited from the *British Quarterly Review*.

137. P. 27. "The terminology, as well as the minute distinctions
of Dr. Schmucker's classification of mental phenomena, are
decidedly objectionable. They tend to bewilder and per-
plex the student, and to retard the progress of sound philosophy." Blakey, *loc. cit.*, pp. 533-4.

"The general theory, and especially the classification and
terminology of Schmucker, have sometimes led him into
hasty, imperfect, and one-sided views and generalizations
. . . [his] application of the word *idea* to feelings—or
sentient states of mind, appears to us highly objectionable.
It seems to involve a confounding of that most important
distinction in mental philosophy—the difference between
the thinking and the feeling—the intellectual and the
sentient parts of our constitution. . . Nor can we regard
his terminology, as a whole, in a more unfavourable light;
it is incorrect, inexpressive, and unhappily chosen. In our
judgment, it fails to answer any of the conditions which
accurate, scientific, or even popular classifications, ought to
fulfil. . . In short, we must confess, that the classification and terminology of Professor Schmucker's system appear to us, on the whole, to be arbitrary, cumbrous, and
confused. They are calculated, in our opinion, to impede
rather than to facilitate the progress of mental science."
British Quarterly Review, pp. 110, 113, 114, 115.

138. "Linberg's translation of Cousin's 'Introduction to the History of Philosophy' may be considered as the great store-
house, from which most of them—e.g., Brownson, Emerson, Parker, etc.—derived their peculiar philosophical
opinions, their mode of reasoning, and their forms of
thought and expression." James Murdock, *op. cit.* See also
Riley, p. 235. The philosophy of Cousin as well as that
of the modern Germans is described by Murdock (cited in
Townsend, Appendix).

139. S. T. Coleridge, 1772-1834. "Biographia Literaria," about
1817, quoted by Upham; "Aids to Reflection," 1825;
"The Friend," 1812-, edited by H. N. Coleridge, 1844

(full details in Allibone). R. W. Emerson visited Coleridge in 1833, but "meanwhile in an adjoining state there had been issued an American edition of the 'Aids to Reflection' with a competent introduction by President Marsh, and it was this work which did most to introduce the modified German philosophy into our country." Riley, p. 170. See both Riley and Townsend, *passim.*

140. 1799-1869. Born at Vernon, N. Y. Graduated from Hamilton College in 1824, and from Andover Theological Seminary in 1827. Pastor at Pittsford, N. Y., and in Cincinnati, until in 1835 he became the first President of Oberlin College, founded in 1833. Here he made educational history by opening the college to all students, irrespective of race, creed, color, *or sex.* In 1850 he resigned to become President of the ill-fated Cleveland University. After an interim he returned to college work, becoming Professor and later President (1860-71) of Adrian College. He spent the latter years of his long and active life in England. "Dict. of Am. Biog.," with bibliography.

141. Oberlin, 1840, 305 pp.; mental philosophy, pp. 9-168.

142. First Ed., N. Y., 1845, 330 pp.; 2nd Ed., 1854, 476 pp. "Some of the most important chapters have been so entirely rewritten and remodeled, as to render the present, in some important respects, a new work." Prefatory Note to the Revised Edition.

143. "Doctrine of the Will," N. Y., 1845 (copyrighted 1844), 218 pp. The next citation is from this volume.

144. After a critique of the method of Locke, Stewart, Reid, etc., and Abercrombie, he announces the true method (following Cousin): (1) "Mark the phenomena actually existing in the mind at the present moment—classify and arrange these phenomena, and carefully mark their characteristics. (2) The powers or faculties indicated by these phenomena. (3) The operation of these powers including these phenomena in their origin, genesis, and final development. (4) Ontology. (5) God and the Infinite. (6) The relations of of the finite to the infinite, etc., morality, etc." "Abstract," p. 11.

145. "Abstract," pp. 174-188.
146. Prefatory Note to the Revised Edition of the "Intellectual Philosophy." See pp. 331-404 for the complete exposition.
147. The Preface to the Second Edition (1854) reads: "Since the publication of the first edition of this work [N. B., 1845], the author has had the benefit resulting from successive years in teaching the same, and of a careful *reading of other works* upon the same subject [italics mine]. . . Some of the most important chapters have been entirely rewritten . . among others, the Chapter on Sense. . . The author has always been fully persuaded of the correctness of his views in respect to external perception, but has felt a growing dissatisfaction with his manner of presenting the subject. . . In the present edition, this subject, so fundamental to a right system of mental science, is so presented as to meet his ideas in most, if not all respects."

The "other works upon the same subject," according to the custom of the time, are not specified, but internal evidence points conclusively to Hamilton's Edition of "Reid's Works," 1846, particularly the scholarly notes on Perception at the end of the second volume. This 1854 revision in the light of Hamilton's exposition of perception marks dramatically the exact moment of the beginning of the great influence that Hamilton was to have upon American psychology.

148. 1809-1877. Born in the wilds of Kentucky. Graduated from West Point in 1830. Professor of Mathematics at Kenyon (1833-4) and at Miami (1835-6), and then practiced law at Springfield, publishing his "Examination of President Edwards' Inquiry into the Freedom of the Will" (Philadelphia, 1845, 234 pp.) during this period. From 1848 to 1854 professor of mathematics at the University of Mississippi, publishing his "Theodicy" in 1853, and from 1854 until the outbreak of the Civil War at the University of Virginia. He was a fiery Southern patriot, becoming a colonel in the Confederate army by virtue of his military training, but later released by President Davis to

devote his brains and his pen to propaganda for the Southern cause. "Dict. of Am. Biog."

149. 1789-1888. Born at Bethel, Conn. Granduated from Union College in 1820. Ordained at Kent, Conn., in 1823, remaining there as pastor for six years. Later pastor at Litchfield, Conn., then from 1836 to 1844 Professor in Western Reserve College, in the Auburn Theological Seminary from 1844 to 1852, then Professor of Mental and Moral Philosophy and Vice-President of Union College from 1852 on, becoming President in 1866. In 1869 he resigned and retired to Amherst to devote himself to literary labors. For many years he was a familiar figure to the students there, as was related personally to the writer by Professor R. S. Woodworth. Both Prof. Woodworth and Professor F. J. E. Woodbridge began their study of psychology from Hickok's "Empirical Psychology." "Dict. of Am. Biog."

150. 1854; 2nd Edition, N. Y., 1871, 400 pp.

151. 1848, Auburn, 717 pp.; 2nd Ed., Boston, 1861 (my own copy reprinted in 1882), 543 pp.

152. From the article in the "Dict. of Am. Biog."; also the characterization at the head of the paragraph.

153. Preface to the 1st Edition of the "Rational Psychology."

154. Preface to the 2nd Ed., p. v. A careful comparison of the two editions is most illuminating.

155. *Ibid.*, p. vi. All the following citations are from the 1st Ed.

156. 1799-1864. Born in Williston, Vt., graduated from Yale in 1825, and studied theology at Andover and at Yale. Was Lyman Beecher's successor in the Bowdoin St. Church, Boston. From 1844 to 1853 he conducted the Mt. Vernon Institute in Boston, and devoted himself to the cause of higher education in Boston and in the colleges. "Moral Philosophy," 1856. "Intellectual Philosophy," 1852; 8th Ed., Boston, 1863, 422 pp. Appleton, "Cyc. of Am. Biog."

157. 1772-1851. Archibald Alexander, born in Rockbridge County, Va. Studied in the Academy of Rev. William Graham, later Washington and Lee University. Was an itinerant pastor for a time, and then in 1796 became President of

Hampden Sidney College. On the reorganization of the Theological Seminary at Princeton in 1812 he became the leading Professor. Died in 1851, leaving the "Moral Science" in manuscript (published in N. Y., 1852, 272 pp.). Appleton, "Cyc. of Am. Biog."

158. N. Y., 1853, 411 pp.

159. 1796-1865. Born in New York City. Graduated from Union College under Eliphalet Nott in 1813. Studied medicine for three years, then theology, later becoming a tutor in Union College. Pastor in Boston from 1821 to 1826. In 1826 he became Professor at Union, resigning in 1827 to become President of Brown University. He remained in that position for 28 years, and effected a complete reorganization in 1850. A prolific writer. Appleton, "Cyc. of Am. Biog." "Elements of Intellectual Philosophy," Boston, 1854; 1855 (7th thousand), 426 pp.

160. The references were compiled by Samuel Brooks and L. W. Bancroft, former pupils of Dr. Wayland, and are mostly to Reid, Stewart, Locke, and Abercrombie, less often to Cousin and Hamilton. Incidental references in the text to Hobbes, Berkeley, Brown, Coleridge, Carpenter, Foster, Butler, and Upham.

161. 1816-1874. Born, Dennis, Mass. Graduated from Amherst in 1835. After some teaching and pastoral experience, became Professor of Mental and Moral Philosophy at Amherst (1850-58), of Theology in the Chicago Theological Seminary (1858-70), resigning to spend some years in foreign travel, and becoming Professor of Mental and Moral Science in the University of Chicago from 1873 to his death. "He was a close student, remarkable for the extent and thoroughness of his scholarship." Appleton, "Dict. of Am. Biog."

162. Boston, 1857. "It soon became the most popular text-book on this subject. . . So great has been the demand for this book, that the stereotyped plates have been entirely worn out, in printing edition after edition." Publishers' note in new edition of 1883, 590 pp.

163. Preface, p. v. See the whole preface for a critique of previous texts in Mental Philosophy.
164. Pp. 585-590, citing 103 authorities. The most useful bibliography since the chapter references in Upham's 1827 work on "Intellectual Philosophy" (Upham discontinued his bibliographies in subsequent editions). It is a severe task to go through any of these books and ascertain with any exactness the direct and indirect references. Bibliographical science is of very recent development. Strictures might be made on books as recent as, for example, Ragsdale, *op. cit.*, 1932, for a complete absence of bibliography, and on most books up to very recent years for incomplete citation of titles, authors, editions consulted, number of pages, etc.

CHAPTER THREE

1. Beard, *op. cit.*, II, p. 415.
2. Schmidt, *op. cit.*, p. 226.
3. Adams, II, p. 154.
4. Snow, *op. cit.*, p. 174.
5. *Ibid.*, p. 162.
6. Beard, II, p. 408.
7. Schmidt, pp. 227-8.
8. "The moral philosophy course began to disintegrate into its component parts. Philosophy, psychology, economics and political science each claimed its share until little was left of the old omnibus course." Schmidt, p. 228.

   "Significant in this connection are the integration and orientation courses that are growing common in colleges and undergraduates departments of universities today. These courses usually represent an attempt to check the disintegration process, which, aggravated by the spread of the free elective system, has in recent years been leading educational curricula into the opposite extreme of excessive diffusion." *Ibid.*, 143. He quotes R. L. Kelly, "The Effective College": "These ancient settees, from which some dear old professor had dispensed prodigious amounts of Latin, astronomy, Bible, geology and mathematics, are being brought down from the attic, carefully dusted, and restored to their places of honor in the classroom." *Ibid.*, p. 144.

9. *Princeton Review*, quoted in Allibone, article "Porter."

10. Boston, 1863, 338 pp.

11. 1807-1881. Born at Beverly, Mass. Graduated from Bowdoin College, 1827. Supt. at Butler (Providence, R. I.) from 1845 to 1866. Allibone lists five major publications, besides contributions to periodicals and annual reports. "He was an accomplished psychiatrist and in those days a giant among men of his specialty." "Dict. of Am. Biog."

12. The term mind is employed as a "generic expression of the mental phenomena without reference to their origin or nature. And so of the term, brain. However I may use it for the sake of convenience, I would not be supposed to favor any theory whatever respecting its connection with the mind" (p. 15).

13. 1803-1885. Born at Onondaga, N. Y. Graduated from Hamilton College in 1828. Professor at Wesleyan College, Middleton, Conn., 1833-43, and at the Univ. of Michigan from 1845-52. Editor of the *Methodist Quarterly Review*, 1856-84. Allibone, Appleton. "The Freedom of the Will," N. Y., 1864, 438 pp.

14. 1801-1888. Born at S. Kingstown, R. I. Allibone, "Dict. of Am. Biog." Brief notice in Townsend, p. 114. "All Mr. Hazard's writings are eminently fresh, acute, and original." Porter in Ueberweg, II, p. 458. "Freedom of the Mind," N. Y., 1864, 455 pp.

15. Boston, 1869.

16. Hazard, p. 166. Cf. Thurstone, L. L., "The Nature of Intelligence," N. Y., Harcourt, Brace, 1924, 167 pp.

17. 1786-1869. Born at Philadelphia. Graduated from Princeton in 1805, and from the Medical School of the Univ. of Penn. in 1809. Studied in Edinburgh, and practiced medicine in Philadelphia, retiring from the profession to devote himself to scientific and literary pursuits. Appleton. "Brief Outline," Phil., 1865, 2 vols., 450 and 480 pp. A rare work.

18. Brett, *op. cit.*, III, pp. 257-8. Brett's knowledge of the work

was probably limited to the comment by Porter in Ueberweg, II, p. 458: "In this work the author teaches, that in connection with every action of the intellect there is a physical action of the senses and the brain." This note, in turn, was probably paraphrased from the review in *Trübner's Amer. and Oriental Record*, Sept. 21, 1865: "This is a very remarkable book, intended to form a natural history of the human intellect. The author proceeds on the assumption that from the beginning to the end of the few and simple functions of the mind there is a physical action of the senses and brain." The exact wording of the sentence in Rush's book from which these illuminating critiques were taken is found on page 3 of Vol. I: "The following method of investigating the mind, from the beginning to the end of its few and simple functions, is conducted on the ground of their being altogether a physical action of the senses and the brain." It is extremely unlikely that the first reviewer read any further, and the tragedy of the whole matter is that the world followed the example of the first reviewer.

19. Dr. Rush has favored the reader with an Appendix to the Second Volume, in which he reviews minutely the steps by which he laid out his theory. It is a most fascinating glimpse into an original mind, and one pardons the garrulity of an old man for the value of the revelation.

20. Allibone, "Dictionary of Authors," article "James Rush." The punctuation sign (;) used in the citations, is the dicomma, invented by Dr. Rush.

21. Wickham, Harvey, "The Misbehaviorists," N. Y., MacVeagh, 1928, 294 pp.

22. Brett, III, p. 258.

23. 1807-1885. Born at Cairo, N. Y. Entered Brown, but transferred to Union, from which he was graduated in 1829, afterwards spending two years at the Princeton Theological Seminary. Was in turn tutor at Princeton, Professor at Williams and at Lafayette, President of Jefferson College (1857-62), and Principal of the State Normal School at Albany (1867-82). He was accounted a great teacher, though an impatient administrator. "His success in the classroom

was largely due to his ability to clarify a subject quickly and reveal the essential facts. A clear thinker himself, he trained his students to think logically." "Dict. of Am. Biog." "Elements," N. Y., 1866, 292 pp.

24. Samuel Bailey, British, 1791-1870, author of "Essays on the Pursuit of Truth and Progress of Knowledge," 1844; "Letters on the Philosophy of the Human Mind," 1855-58, "Theory of Reasoning," 1852, etc. McCosh, "Intuitions of the Mind," 1860 (McCosh had not yet come to America).

25. Pp. 4, 7, 55.

26. 1827-1911. Born at Genoa, N. Y. Graduated from Williams in 1849. Studied in the Auburn Theological Seminary, where he came under the influence of L. P. Hickok. Became tutor, afterwards professor, at Williams, and in 1874 President of the Univ. of Wisconsin, where he made great internal improvements. Resigned in 1887, returned to Williams, remaining there as professor until 1903. "Dict. of Am. Biog." "Principles," N. Y., 1869, 345 pp.; "Science of Mind," N. Y., 1881, 474 pp. Bascom also wrote a "Comparative Psychology," N. Y., 1878, 297 pp., defining his subject as "a knowledge of intelligence, of conscious activity, as it exists in all accessible forms of lives, a tracing of its development in its several stages through the entire animal kingdom" (p. 2). It is rather a genetic than a comparative psychology in the modern use of the word. The list of topics considered gives an insight into the scope and method of the work: Mind and matter, physical forces as related to vital forces, vegetable life, the nervous system, animal life as organic, instinctive, and associative, rational life, the supreme reason.

27. "Dict. of Am. Biog.," article "John Bascom." "Professor Bascom is a vigorous and independent critic." Porter in Ueberweg, II, p. 456.

28. "Comparative Psychology," p. iv.

29. "Science of Mind," p. v. Subsequent citations are all from the "Science of Mind."

30. "Bien qu'influencé par les spéculations de la pensée germanique, auxquelles Porter s'était familiarisé en Allemagne en 1853,

cet ouvrage répond, dans sa conception et ses vues fonda-
mentales, aux doctrines de l'école écossaise." Van Becelaere,
p. 67. "The philosophy taught in this volume is pronounced
and positive in the spiritual and theistic direction, as con-
trasted with the materialistic and anti-theistic tendency which
is so earnestly defended by its advocates as alone worthy
to be called scientific. The author, though earnest in his
opinion, has aimed to adhere most rigidly to the methods
of true science, and to employ no arguments which he did
not believe would endure the closest scrutiny." "Human
Intellect," p. vii. See also article by B. M. Duncan in Merriam, G. E., Ed., "Noah Porter, A Memorial by Friends,"
N. Y., Scribners, 1893, 306 pp.

31. N. Y., 1868; 4th ed., 1891, 673 pp. "The more important
definitions, propositions, and arguments are printed in the
largest type, in distinct paragraphs. . . The matter which
is properly explanatory and illustrative of the leading propositions is printed in smaller type. . . The historical, critical,
and controversial matter is printed in the smallest type, in
which will be found most of that which is especially ab-
struse and metaphysical." Preface, pp. v, vi. "Incomparably
superior to any treatises on psychology in English existing
at the date when it appeared. . . It is a thesaurus of its
subject, containing in outline the results of the best thinking
which had been done in all ages on the human mind." Duncan in Merriam, *op. cit.*, pp. 199-200. The huge work was
abridged as the "Elements of Intellectual Science," N. Y.,
1871, 565 pp., and used as a text in numerous universities,
colleges, academies, normal and high schools.

32. 1811-1892. Born at Farmington, Conn. Graduated from Yale
in 1831. Clark Professor of Moral Philosophy and Metaphysics at Yale, 1846-71, President from 1871-86. Retired
from the Presidency but remained professor until his death.
Spent the year 1853-4 at the University of Berlin. "Dict.
of Am. Biog." See also "Noah Porter, A Memorial."

33. Riley, "American Thought," p. 239.

34. Townsend, pp. 101-2.

35. Brett, III, pp. 258-9.

36. Van Becelaere, pp. 67, 68-9.
37. Van Becelaere, p. 67.
38. *Ibid.*, p. 68.
39. 1811-1882. President of Waterville College from 1857 to
    1873. Appleton, "Text-book of Intellectual Philosophy,"
    Boston, 1870 (Porter in Ueberweg says 1860); New Edi-
    tion, Remodeled, N. Y., 1874, 314 pp., containing an
    admirable little abstract of the history of philosophy, ex-
    planatory notes, and questions on the text. Allibone calls
    Champlin "a distinguished classical scholar."
40. "A Textbook in Psychology," N. Y., 1871, 320 pp. (Copy
    in Columbia Library.)
41. 1816-1900. "Lectures on the Psychology of Thought and Ac-
    tion, Comparative and Human," Ithaca, 1871, 300 pp.
    (Copy in Union Theological Seminary Library.) Among
    other works Professor Wilson wrote a "Logic," 1856, which
    Porter (in Ueberweg, II) compliments very highly, and in
    1877, a work entitled "Live Questions in Psychology and
    Metaphysics."
42. Originally published in 1848; Second Edition, 1849, a duo-
    decimo of 175 pp.; in its final form, N. Y., 1872, 707 pp.
    It purports to afford "reliable evidence of the existence of
    the Soul as an independent, self-acting, immortal, and spir-
    itual essence." Preface to the 1849 edition. "The Narratives
    of Creation and the Flood will be shown, demonstratively,
    to be literally direct revelations by the Creator, and that they
    were intended to be received in their obvious sense. The
    former is immediately related to our main purpose of estab-
    lishing the substantive existence of the Soul as a self-acting
    agent, and a principle of life, as distinguished from external
    forces, or as the functional results of the organic mechanism;
    for it is expressly affirmed that 'The Lord God formed man
    of the dust of the ground, and breathed into his nostrils
    the breath of life; and man became a living Soul.' 'So God
    created man in his Own Image; in the Image of God cre-
    ated He him.' . . In regard to the Narrative of the Flood,
    a primary object of the demonstration of its Divine Revela-

tion is that of showing how it goes to sustain our position in relation to the Soul." Edition of 1872, p. ix.

43. 1794-1877. Born in Vermont; A.B. and M.D., Harvard. From 1841 to 1867 Professor in the Medical School of the University of New York, which he founded. Among 14 works listed, Dr. Paine was the author of "The Institutes of Medicine," 1847; 9th ed., 1870, 1,151 pp., most highly commended.

44. Brett, III, p. 258.

45. Bernard, L. L., "Instinct, A Study in Social Psychology," N. Y., Holt, 1924, 550 pp.

46. 1823-1883. "Dict. of Am. Biog." "Instinct, Its Office in the Animal Kingdom and its Relation to the Higher Powers of Man," N. Y., 1872.

47. Murphy, p. 336. See the whole chapter, pp. 336-346.

48. Boston, 1873 (copyright 1872), 701 pp.

49. 1802-1887. Born at Stockbridge, Mass. Graduated at Williams, 1824; tutor at Williams for two years, then professor from 1830 until his death, serving as President from 1836 to 1872. "Dict. of Am. Biog." "President Hopkins is singularly independent and individual in his methods of thinking and writing." Porter in Ueberweg, II, p. 456.

50. "An Outline Study of Man; or, The Body and Mind in one System, with Illustrative Diagrams, and a Method for Blackboard Teaching," N. Y., 1878, 308 pp., with folded insert.

51. N. Y., "Lowell Lectures on Moral Science," Boston, 1862; "The Law of Love" (Lowell Lectures, 2nd series), N. Y., 1869; 3rd edition, 1871; revised edition for use with "Outline Study of Man," N. Y., 1886, including in an Appendix the debate with McCosh. On the Appendix Porter comments (*ibid. ut supra*) that it "is very instructive, as exhibiting the author's theory, which may be described as a combination of Jonathan Edwards and that of Jouffroy, in contrast with that of Reid and Price, as defended by Dr. McCosh."

52. Lecture I, pp. 1-25.

53. Pp. 14-15, 21. Cf. Morgan, C. L., "Emergent Evolution," N. Y., Holt, 1928, 313 pp.

54. 1808-1890. Professor at Western Reserve College, 1840-58, and President of Ohio Female College, 1858-64. "Dict. of Am. Biog." "Elements of Psychology," N. Y., 1876, 248 pp.

55. 1828-1913. "Empirical and Rational Psychology," Cincinnati, 1882, 484 pp., pp. 241-413 being a complete course in Logic, given in response to "a growing demand, by progressive teachers, to have Logic presented in connection with Psychology" (p. iv). "Psychology treats directly of Cognition, Feeling, and Volitions, and indirectly of Intellect, Sensibility, and Will. Greater prominence is thus given to the phenomena of the soul, with their conditions and laws, than to the faculties implied by these phenomena." "Though much light has, no doubt, been thrown upon Psychology by the investigations of Physiologists, . . . yet . . . it will not suffice to examine the structure and functions of the nerves, the ganglia, the brain, and the organs of sense . . . to know any phenomenon, as it is in itself, we must study it in consciousness" (p. iii). A fine history and critique of Theories of Perception, pp. 156-194. A sane and well-written text. A rare book, the copy I have examined being the property of the University of Rochester, presented by David Jayne Hill.

56. 1834-1918. Born in Belfast, Ireland. Came to America with his father in 1843. Graduated from Hanover College in 1833, attended Princeton Theological Seminary for a year, then Union and New Albany Seminaries, returning to Princeton to spend the years 1856-58. After some pastoral experience, became Professor of Mental Philosophy at Hanover College, was acting Professor at Princeton, then Professor at Hamilton College in 1884, resigning in 1891 to devote himself to various literary and teaching pursuits until his death in Plainfield, N. J. "Dict. of Am. Biog."

57. N. Y., 1882, 720 pp.; reissued as "Mental Science," N. Y., 1885, 416 pp.; again in 1899, with the title changed to "The Perceptionalist"; reprinted in 1912, 411 pp., part of the work being in fine print, allowing of two somewhat independent courses of instruction.

58. By Professor S. Stanhope Orris, Professor of Greek and Latin Philosophy at Princeton.

59. "The Perceptionalist," 1912, pp. xi, xviii. Subsequent citations from the same ed.

60. Van Becelaere, p. 56.

61. Hall, S. R., "Lectures on Schoolkeeping," Hanover, N. H., Dartmouth Press, Facsimile Reprint, 1929, 141 pp., with life of Hall, 33 pp. Hall opened "the first teacher-training school in America," and his book was "the first professional book in English and intended primarily for teachers." Cubberley, pp. 375, 376.

62. Abbott, Jacob, "The Teacher," Boston, Peirce, 1833, 285 pp. Went through 25 editions by 1860. Cubberley, p. 325.

63. Page, David, "Theory and Practice of Teaching," Syracuse, 1847, Hall and Dickson, 349 pp. Went through countless editions and reprints, and was still on a Reading Circle list in 1884-5 (together with Watt's "Improvement of the Mind"). B. A. Hinsdale in "Education in the U. S.," N. M. Butler, editor, Albany, Lyon, 1900, 2 vols., 972 pp., pp. 359-408.

64. Boston, 1887 (copyright 1886).

65. Thorndike, E. L., "Educational Psychology," N. Y., Lemcke and Buchner, 1903.

66. Pyle, W. H., "Outlines of Educational Psychology," Baltimore, Warwick and York, 1911, 254 pp.

67. 1831-1912. Principal at Millersville from 1866 to 1886. Author of books on teaching, and of a series of mathematics texts. "Mental Science," Philadelphia, 1883 (copyright 1882), 504 pp.

68. 1811-1894. Born in Scotland and educated at Glasgow and Edinburgh. After an active career as pastor he became Professor of Logic and Metaphysics in Belfast, 1852-68, leaving to become President of Princeton exactly 100 years after his fellow countryman, John Witherspoon. President 1868-88, then President Emeritus until his death. "Dict. of Am. Biog." "Psychology;" Vol. I, "The Cognitive Powers., N. Y., 1886, 245 pp.; Vol. II, "The Motive Powers," N. Y., 1887, 267 pp. McCosh had already published in 1880 a valuable book on "The Emotions," N. Y., 252 pp.

69. 1847-1910. Graduated 1871 from the University of the City

of New York. Studied in Europe. Became Head of the
Department of Philosophy of Boston University in 1876,
remaining in that position for thirty-five years, and serving
as Dean of the Graduate School. He was influenced greatly
by Lotze, but as the writer of the article in the "Dict. of
Am. Biog." says: "Bowne was no man's understudy." Discussed by Townsend, 153 ff. "Introduction to Psychological
Theory," N. Y., 1886, 329 pp. One is interested to see by
the advertising notes in the back of the 1887 printing that
Abercrombie's "Intellectual Powers" and Upham's "Mental
Philosophy" were still offered for sale.

70. N. Y., 1887, 696 pp. *Vide infra.*
71. "Dict. of Am. Biog.," article "Ladd."
72. 1859-. See "American Men of Science." "Psychology," N. Y.,
    1885, 427 pp. Discussed by Brett, III, pp. 259-261.
73. Vol. I, No. 1, Nov., 1887.
74. Bowne, pp. 298-318, citation from p. 316.
75. "Principles," I, Ch. 10, citation from p. 350.
76. 1850-1932. Born, Plainfield, N. J. Graduated, 1874, from the
    University of Lewisburg (now Bucknell); Professor there,
    then President; President of the University of Rochester,
    1888-1896. Entered the diplomatic service, and wrote "A
    History of Diplomacy" in the International Development
    of Europe. "Elements of Psychology," N. Y., 1888, 419 pp.

CHRONOLOGICAL TABLE OF AMERICAN WORKS AND FOREIGN SOURCES

THE principal American contributions to psychology before 1890, direct and indirect (moral philosophy, ethics, logic, etc.), are given in the first column below with dates of publication. In the second column will be found foreign works quoted or referred to in the American writings. Foreign works printed in capitals and small capitals were used as texts in the colonial colleges, and the earliest known dates for their use are given.

FIRST PERIOD

THEOLOGY AND MORAL PHILOSOPHY (1640-1776)

1. English Scholastic Education (1640-1714)

Before 1600 A.D.

Plato, Aristotle; the Greek and Roman classics, particularly Cicero and Seneca; the Church Fathers, notably St. Augustine; Ramus, Burgersdicius, Calvin's Institutes

1605   Bacon, "Advancement of Learning" (copy in J. Harvard's Library)

1620   Bacon, "Novum Organum"

1623   Ames, "MEDULLA THEOLOGIAE" (Harvard, 1690)

1626   Wollebius, "DIVINITY" (H., 1690)

1630   Ames, "DE CONSCIENTIA" (H., 1690)

1637   Descartes, "Discours de la Methode"

1647   Gassendi, "De Vita, Moribus et Doctrina Epicuri"

1650   Descartes, "Traite des Passions de l'Ame"

1650   Hobbes, "Human Nature"

1651   Hobbes, "Leviathan"

1662   "Port Royal Logic"

1666   More, "ENCHIRIDION ETHICUM" (H., 1690)

1672   Cumberland, "De Legibus Naturae"

1674   Malebranche, "Recherche de la Verite"

1677   Spinoza, "Ethica"
1678   Cudworth, "Intellectual System"
1690   Locke, "Essay" (Yale, 1739-1824; reached America in
        1714)
1691   Geulincx, "Metaphysica"
1695   Leibniz, "Philosophical Works"

1701   Norris, "Ideal World"
1705   Clarke, "Demonstration"
1705   Mandeville, "Fable of the Bees"
1709   Berkeley, "New Theory of Vision"
1710   Berkeley, "Principles of Human Knowledge"
1711   Shaftesbury, "Characteristics"
1713   Berkeley, "Three Dialogues"
1713   Collier, "Clavis Universalis"

2. *The American Enlightenment (1714-1776)*

1724   Crousaz, "Art of Thinking" (Eng. Translation)
1725   Watts, "Logic" (Yale, 1735)
1725   Wollaston, "Religion of Nature Delineated" (Yale,
        1746)
1726   Butler, "Sermons"
1729   Browne, "Human Understanding"
1731   King, "Origin of Evil"
1732   Buffier, "Premières Vérités"
1732   Wolff, "Psychologia Empirica"
1733   Baxter, "Nature of the Human Soul"
1734   Wolff, "Psychologia Rationalis"
1735   *Brattle,* "Logic" (H., 1735; in ms. probably as early as
        1696)
1736   Butler, "Analogy" (H., 1825)
1739   Hume, "Treatise"
1740   Turnball, "Moral Philosophy"
1741   Watts, "Improvement of the Mind" (Princeton, 1750)
1745   Mason, "Self Knowledge"
1746   Condillac, "Essai"
1748   Hume, "Enquiry"
1748   La Mettrie, "l'Homme Machine"

1748   Duncan, "LOGIC" (Yale, 1774)
1749   Hartley, "Observations on Man"
1752   *Johnson*, "ELEMENTA PHILOSOPHICA" (Kings, 1754)
1754   *Edwards*, "FREEDOM OF THE WILL" (Yale, 1761)
1764   Fordyce, "MORAL PHILOSOPHY" (Penn., 1765)
1754   Condillac, "Traité des Sensations"
1755   Hutcheson, "SYSTEM" (Penn., 1756)
1755   Grove, "Moral Philosophy"
1758   Helvetius, "de l'Esprit"
1759   A. Smith, "MORAL SENTIMENTS" (P., 1820)
1760   Bonnet, "Essai"
1762   Kames, "ELEMENTS OF CRITICISM" (Brown, 1774)
1763   Tucker, "Light of Nature"
1763   Doddridge, "LECTURES" (Kings, 1783)
1764   Reid, "INQUIRY"
1765   *Clap*, "ETHICS" (Yale, 1765)
1765   Leibniz, "Nouveaux Essais" (date of publication)
1770   *Dana*, "Examination of Edwards"
1770   Beattie, "Essay on Truth"
1770   d'Holbach, "Système de la Nature"
1776   Campbell, "PHILOSOPHY OF RHETORIC" (Brown, 1827)

SECOND PERIOD

INTELLECTUAL PHILOSOPHY (1776-1861)

1. *Scottish Philosophy (1776-1827)*

1777   Priestley, "Matter and Spirit"
1871   Kant, "Kritik der Reinen Vernunft"
1783   Blair, "RHETORIC" (H., 1785)
1785   Reid, "INTELLECTUAL POWERS"
1785   Ferguson, "Moral and Political Science"
1788   Paley, "MORAL AND POLITICAL PHILOSOPHY" (Yale, 1791)
1788   Reid, "ACTIVE POWERS"
1789   Bentham, "Morals and Legislation"
1790   Beattie, "MORAL SCIENCE"
1790   Alison, "Taste"

1792   Stewart, "ELEMENTS" (Yale, 1824)
1795   *Gros*, "NATURAL PRINCIPLES OF RECTITUDE" (Col., 1795)
1795   *West*, "Liberty and Necessity"
1796   *Edwards, Jr.*, "Liberty and Necessity" (answer to West)

1800   Cogan, "Treatise on the Passions"
1800   Fichte, "Science of Knowledge"
1800   *Witherspoon*, "MORAL PHILOSOPHY" (P., lecture notes, from 1768)
1801   Belsham, "Philosophy of the Human Mind"
1802   Paley, "NATURAL THEOLOGY"
1802   De Gerando, "Connaissances Humaines"
1804-6   Sidney Smith, "Moral Philosophy"
1806   Scott, "Intellectual Philosophy"
1806   Hegel, "Phenomenologie"
1810   *Smith*, "Essay"
1812   de Biran, "Essai"
1812   *Rush*, "Diseases of the Mind"
1812   *Smith*, "MORAL AND POLITICAL PHILOSOPHY" (P., from 1794)
1816   Herbart, "Lehrbuch"
1816   *Hedge*, "LOGIC"
1817   Coleridge, "Biographica Litteraria"
1819   *Ely*, "Conversations on the Science of the Human Mind"
1820   Brown, "LECTURES" (H., 1825)
1820   *Baylies*, "Free Agency of Man"
1822   *Beasley*, "Search for Truth"
1823   Taylor, "Elements of Thought"
1824   *Burton*, "Metaphysics, Ethics and Theology"
1824   Combe, "Phrenology"
1825   Jardine, "Philosophical Education"
1826   Cousin, "Fragments Philosophiques"
1826   Whately, "Logic"
1826   *Reed*, "Observations on the Growth of the Mind"

2. *American Textbooks (1827-1861)*

1827   *Upham*, "INTELLECTUAL PHILOSOPHY"
1828   Combe, "Constitution of Man"

1828   Stewart, "ACTIVE AND MORAL POWERS"
1828   Payne, "Mental and Moral Science"
1828   *Anon.*, "Mental Guide"
1829   Blaisdale, "Intellectual Philosophy"
1829   Hamilton, Articles in the Edinburgh Review
1829   J. Mill, "Analysis of the Human Mind"
1829   Taylor, "Enthusiasm"
1830   Abercrombie, "Intellectual Powers"
1830   Burder, "Mental Discipline"
1830   Mackintosh, "Progress of Ethical Philosophy"
1831   *Upham*, "MENTAL PHILOSOPHY"
1833   Abercrombie, "Moral Feelings"
1833   Beneke, "Lehrbuch"
1833   Wardlaw, "Christian Ethics"
1834   *Upham*, "WILL"
1834   Young, "Intellectual Philosophy"
1834   Weber, "De Tactu"
1834   Brougham, "Natural Theology"
1835   *Wayland*, "MORAL SCIENCE"
1836   *Fowler Brothers*, "Phrenology"
1837   *Wayland*, "POLITICAL SCIENCE"
1837   Whewell, "Inductive Sciences"
1838   *Day*, "Will"
1839   *Sawyer*, "Mental Philosophy"
1839   *Ricord*, "Philosophy of Mind"
1839   Coleridge, "Aids to Reflection"
1839   *Tappan*, "Will" (3 vols., 1839, 1840, 1841)
1840   *Upham*, "Disordered Mental Action"
1840   *Mahan*, "Abstract"
1840   *Rauch*, "Psychology"
1841   *Day*, "Examination of Edwards"
1842   Thompson, "Laws of Thought"
1842   *Schmucker*, "Psychology"
1842   *Fiske*, "Mental Philosophy"
1843   Combe, "Moral Philosophy"
1843   J. S. Mill, "System of Logic"
1845   *Mahan*, "Intellectual Philosophy"
1845   *Mahan*, "Doctrine of the Will"

1845   *Bledsoe,* "Examination of Edwards"
1845   Moore, "Power of the Soul over the Body"
1845   Feuchtersleben, "Medical Psychology"
1846   Hamilton, "Reid's Works with Notes"
1846   Weber, "Tastsinn and Gemeingefühl"
1846   *Richards,* "Mental Philosophy"
1848   *Hickok,* "Rational Psychology"
1849   Whately, "Rhetoric"
1850   *Haddock,* "Psychology"
1850   *Lord,* "Anthroposophy"
1852   *Winslow,* "Intellectual Philosophy"
1852   Lotze, "Medicinische Psychologie"
1852   *Alexander,* "Moral Science"
1854   *Wayland,* "Intellectual Philosophy"
1854   *Hickok,* "Empirical Psychology"
1855   *Bowen,* "Metaphysics and Ethical Science"
1855   *Rush,* "Philosophy of the Human Voice"
1855   *Tappan,* "Logic"
1855   Spencer, "Psychology"
1855   Bain, "Senses and Intellect"
1856   Helmholtz, "Physiologische Optik"
1857   *Haven,* "Mental Philosophy"
1857   *Carleton,* "Liberty and Necessity"
1859   Darwin, "Origin of Species"
1859   Bain, "Emotions and Will"
1859   Whately, "Lessons on Mind"
1859   Hamilton, "Metaphysics"
1859   *Taylor,* "Moral Government"
1860   *Collins,* "Humanics"
1860   McCosh, "Intuitions of the Mind"
1860   Fechner, "Psychophysics"

THIRD PERIOD

BRITISH AND GERMAN INFLUENCE (1861-1890)

1862   Mansel, "Artis Logicae Rudimenta"
1862   Helmholtz, "Tonempfindungen"
1863   *Ray,* "Mental Hygiene"

1864 *Hazard*, "Freedom of the Mind in Willing"
1864 *Whedon*, "Freedom of the Will"
1865 *Rush*, "Analysis of the Human Intellect"
1865   J. S. Mill, "Hamilton's Philosophy"
1866 *Alden*, "Intellectual Philosophy"
1867   Maudsley, "Physiology and Pathology of Mind"
1868 *Porter*, "Human Intellect"
1869 *Bascom*, "Principles of Psychology"
1869   Galton, "Hereditary Genius"
1869   Taine, "l'Intelligence"
1870 *Champlin*, "Intellectual Philosophy"
1871   Darwin, "Descent of Man"
1871 *Wilson*, "Psychology of Thought and Action"
1871 *Munsell*, "Psychology"
1871 *Paine*, "Physiology of the Soul and Instinct"
1872 *Hamilton, D. H.*, "Autology"
1872 *Chadbourne*, "Instinct"
1872   Darwin, "Expression of the Emotions"
1873   Wundt, "Physiologische Psychologie"
1874   Brentano, "Psychologie"
1875   Carpenter, "Mental Physiology"
1876 *Day*, "Elements of Psychology"
1878 *Hopkins*, "Outline Study of Man"
1878 *Bascom*, "Comparative Psychology"
1880 *McCosh*, "Emotions"
1881   Preyer, "Mind of the Child"
1882 *Schuyler*, "Empirical and Rational Psychology"
1882 *Brooks*, "Mental Culture"
1882 *Hamilton, E. J.*, "The Human Mind"
1883   Galton, "Human Faculty"
1884   Sully, "Outlines of Psychology"
1885   Ebbinghaus, "Gedächtniss"
1885   Mach, "Analyse der Empfindungen"
1886   Ward, Article in the Encyclopaedia Britannica
1886   Binet, "Psychologie du Raisonnement"
1886 *McCosh*, "Psychology"
1886 *Bowne*, "Psychological Theory"
1886 *Dewey*, "Psychology"

1886 *Hopkins*, "The Law of Love"
1886   Sully, "Teacher's Handbook of Psychology"
1887 *Ladd*, "Physiological Psychology"
1888 *Hill*, "Elements of Psychology"
1889 *Baldwin*, "Handbook"
1889 *Hewett*, "Elements of Psychology"
1890 *James*, "Principles of Psychology"

BIBLIOGRAPHY OF PRIMARY SOURCES IN AMERICAN PSYCHOLOGY BEFORE 1890

Alden, J., "Elements of Intellectual Philosophy," N. Y., Appleton, 1866, 292 pp.

Alexander, A., "Outlines of Moral Science," N. Y., Scribner, 1852, 272 pp.

Anon., "The Mental Guide," Boston, Marsh and Capen, 1828, 384 pp.

Baldwin, J. M., "Handbook of Psychology," N. Y., Holt, Vol. I, 1889. "Senses and Intellect" (Vol. II, 1891, "Feeling and Will").

Bascom, J., "Comparative Psychology; or, The Growth and Grades of Intelligence," N. Y., Putnam, 1878, 297 pp.

Baylies, N., "An Essay Concerning the Free Agency of Man," Montpelier, Walton, 1820, 215 pp.

Beasley, F., "A Search for Truth in the Science of the Human Mind," Philadelphia, Potter, 1822, 561 pp.

Bledsoe, A. T., "An Examination of President Edwards' Inquiry into the Freedom of the Will," Phil., Hooker, 1845, 234 pp.

Bowen, F., "Principles of Metaphysical and Ethical Science," Boston, Brewer and Tillotson, 1855, 487 pp.

Bowne, B. P., "Introduction to Psychological Theory," N. Y., Harper, 1886, 329 pp.

Brattle, W., "Compendium Logicae," Boston, Draper, 1735, 1758, 60 pp.

Brooks, E., "Mental Science," Phil., Normal Pub. Co., 1882, 503 pp.

Burton, Asa, "Essays on Some of the First Principles of Metaphysicks, Ethicks, and Theology," Portland, Mirror Office, 1824, 414 pp.

Carleton, H., "Liberty and Necessity (In which are considered the laws of Association of Ideas)," Phil., Parry and McMillan, 1857, 165 pp.

Chadbourne, P. A., "Instinct," N. Y., Putnam, 1872, 307 pp.

Champlin, J. T., "Text-Book of Intellectual Philosophy," 1870; N. Y., Potter, Ainsworth, New Edition Remodeled, 1874, 314 pp.

Collins, T. W., "Humanics," N. Y., Appleton, 1860, 358 pp.

Clap, T., "An Essay on the Nature and Foundation of Moral Virtue and Obligation," New Haven, Mecom, 1765, 66 pp.

Dana, J., "An Examination of the late Reverend President Edwards's Enquiry on Freedom of Will," Boston, Kneeland, 1770, 140 pp.

Day, H. N., "Elements of Psychology," N. Y., Putnam, 1876, 248 pp.

Day, J., "An Examination of Pres. Edwards's Inquiry on the Freedom of the Will," New Haven, Durrie and Peck, 1841, 340 pp.

Day, J., "An Inquiry respecting the Self-Determining Power of the Will," New Haven, Herrick and Noyes, 1836, 200 pp.

Dewey, J., "Psychology," N. Y., Harper, 1886, 427 pp.

Edwards, J., "On the Freedom of the Will," 1754; N. Y., Leavitt and Allen, 1857, 190 pp. "Works," S. E. Dwight, Ed., N. Y., Converse, 1829, 10 vols. Vol. I, Life of Edwards.

Edwards, J. (son of the above), "Works," T. Edwards, Ed., Andover, Allen, Morrill and Wardwell, 1842, 2 vols., Vol. I, pp. 295-468, Dissertation concerning Liberty and Necessity, written between 1796 and 1799.

Fiske, N. W., "Outlines of Mental Philosophy and Psychology, In a Series of Questions," Amherst, J. S., and C. Adams, 1842, 72 pp.

Fowler, O. S., and L. N., and Kirkham, S., "Phrenology, Proved, Illustrated and Applied," N. Y., Fowler Bros., 1836; 13th Ed., 1842, 430 pp.

Gros, J. D., "Natural Principles of Rectitude," N. Y., T. and J. Swords, 1795, 456 pp.

Haddock, J., "Psychology," N. Y., Fowler and Wells, 1850, 112 pp.

Hamilton, D. H., "Autology," Boston, Lee and Shepard, 1872, 701 pp.

Hamilton, E. J., "The Human Mind," N. Y., Carter, 1882, 720 pp.

Hamilton, E. J., "Mental Science," N. Y., Carter, 1885, 416 pp. (Reprinted in 1885 as the "Perceptionalist"; New Ed., 1899; Reprint, 1912, 416 pp.)

Haven, J., "Mental Philosophy," Boston, Gould and Lincoln, 1857; New Ed., N. Y., Sheldon, 1883, 590 pp.

Haven, J., "Moral Philosophy," Boston, Gould and Lincoln, 1859, 336 pp.

Hazard, R. C., "Freedom of the Mind in Willing," N. Y., Appleton, 1862, 455 pp.

Hedge, L., "Elements of Logic," 1816; 3rd ed., 1821, Stereotyped, N. Y., Armstrong, 1849, 178 pp.

Hewett, E. C., "Elements of Psychology," Cincinnati, Van Antwerp, Bragg, 1889, 192 pp.

Hickok, L. P., "Empirical Psychology," N. Y., Ivison, Blakeman, Taylor, 1854; 2nd ed., 1871, 400 pp.

Hickok, L. P., "Rational Psychology," Auburn, Derby, Miller, 1848, 717 pp.

Hickok, L. P., "A System of Moral Science," N. Y., Ivison, Blakeman, Taylor, 1853; 3rd ed., 1874, 411 pp.

Hill, D. J., "The Elements of Psychology," N. Y., Sheldon, 1888, 419 pp.

Hopkins, M., "The Law of Love," N. Y., Scribner, rev. ed., 1886, 384 pp.

Hopkins, M., "An Outline Study of Man," N. Y., Scribner, 1878, 308 pp.

Johnson, S., "Elementa Philosophica," Phil., B. Franklin, 1752; in Schneider, S. Johnson, Vol. II, pp. 357-518.

Ladd, G. T., "Elements of Physiological Psychology," N. Y., Scribner, 1887, 696 pp.

Lord, J., "Athanatius versus Mundi, Essays upon Anthroposophy," Portland, Foster and Gerrish, 1850, 30 pp.

McCosh, J., "The Emotions," N. Y., Scribner, 1880, 255 pp.

McCosh, J., "Psychology, The Cognitive Powers," N. Y., Scribner, 1886, 245 pp.; "The Motive Powers," N. Y., Scribner, 1887, 267 pp.

Mahan, A., "Abstract of a Course of Lectures on Mental and Moral Philosophy," Oberlin, Steele, 1841, 305 pp.

Mahan, A., "Doctrine of the Will," N. Y., Newman, 1844, 218 pp.

Mahan, A., "A System of Intellectual Philosophy," N. Y., Saxton and Miles, 1845, 330 pp.; 2nd ed., N. Y., Barnes, 1854, 476 pp.

Munsell, O. S., "Psychology," N. Y., Appleton, 1871, 320 pp.

Paine, M., "Physiology of the Soul and Instinct," N. Y., Harper, 1871, 707 pp.

Peabody, A. P., "A Manual of Moral Philosophy," N. Y., Am. Book Co., 1873, 225 pp.

Porter, N., "The Human Intellect," N. Y., Scribner, 1868, 673 pp.

Ray, I., "Mental Hygiene," Boston, Ticknor and Fields, 1863, 338 pp.

Rauch, F. A., "Psychology," N. Y., Dodd, 1840; 2nd ed., 1841, 401 pp.

Reed, S., "Observations on the Growth of the Mind," Boston, Cummings and Hilliard, 1826, 44 pp.

Richards, J., "Lectures on Mental Philosophy and Theology," N. Y., Dodd, 501 pp.

Ricord, E., "Philosophy of the Mind," Geneva, Bogert, 1839, 408 pp.

Rush, B., "Medical Inquiries and Observations on the Diseases of the Mind," Phil., Kimber and Richardson, 1812, 367 pp.; Vol. I (of 4 vol. set), Phil., 1st ed., 1789-98; 3rd, 1809, Johnson and Warner, 456 pp.

Rush, B., "Sixteen Introductory Lectures to Course of Lectures upon the Institutes and Practice of Medicine, with Two Lectures upon the Pleasures of the Senses and of the Mind with an Inquiry into their Proximate Cause," Phil., 1811, Bradford and Innskeep, 455 pp.

Rush, J., "Brief Outline of an Analysis of the Human Intellect," Phil., 1865, 2 vols., Lippincott, 450, 480 pp.

Rush, J., "The Philosophy of the Human Voice," Phil., Lippincott, Grambo, 1855; 4th ed., 559 pp.

Sawyer, L. A., "Mental Philosophy," New Haven, Durrie and Peck, 1839, 316 pp.

Schmucker, S. S., "Psychology," N. Y., Harper, 1842; 2nd ed., 1855, 329 pp.

Schuyler, A., "Empirical and Rational Psychology," Cincinnati, Van Antwerp, Bragg, 1882, 484 pp.

Smith, S. S., "An Essay on the Causes of the Variety of Complexion and Figure in the Human Species," New Brunswick, Simpson, 1810, 411 pp.

Smith, S. S., "Lectures on Moral and Political Philosophy," Trenton, Fenton, 1812, 2 vols., Vol. I, 324 pp.

Tappan, H. P., "Elements of Logic," N. Y., Appleton, 1855, 467 pp.

Tappan, H. P., "Review of Edwards," N. Y., Wiley and Putnam, 1839, 300 pp. "Doctrine of the Will determined by an Appeal to Consciousness," N. Y., W. and P., 1840, 318 pp. "Doctrine of the Will applied to Moral Agency and Responsibility," W. and P., 1841, 348 pp.

Taylor, N. W., "Lectures on the Moral Government of God," N. Y., Clark, Austin and Smith, 1859, 2 vols., 417, 423 pp.

Upham, T. C., "Elements of Intellectual Philosophy," Portland, Shirley and Hyde, copyright, 1827; 2nd ed., 1828, 576 pp.

Upham, T. C., "Elements of Mental Philosophy," Boston, Wells and Lily, 1831, 2 vols.; new ed., Harper, 1869, 561, 705 pp.

Upham, T. C., "A Philosophical and Practical Treatise on the Will," Portland, Hyde, 1834, 400 pp.

Upham, T. C., "Outline of Imperfect and Disordered Mental Action," N. Y., Harper, 1840, 399 pp.

Wayland, F., "Elements of Intellectual Philosophy," Boston, Phillips, Sampson, 1854, 426 pp.

Wayland, F., "Elements of Moral Science," Boston, Gould, Kendall and Lincoln, 1835; 4th ed., 1847, 396 pp.

West, Samuel, "Essays on Liberty and Necessity," New Bedford, Spooner, 1795, 96 pp.

Whedon, D. D., "Freedom of the Will," N. Y., Carlton and Potter, 1864, 438 pp.

Wilson, W. D., "Lectures on the Psychology of Thought and Action, Comparative and Human," Ithaca, Andrus, McChain and Lyons, 1871, 300 pp.

Winslow, H., "Elements of Intellectual Philosophy," 1852; Boston, Brewer and Tileston, 1861, 8th ed., 442 pp.

Witherspoon, J., "Lectures on Moral Philosophy," in Vol. III of "Works," pp. 268-374, Phil., Woodward, 1800. Reprinted, V. L. Collins, Ed., Princeton, Princeton Univ. Press, 1912, 144 pp.

INDEX OF NAMES